To Tessa and Kits

ACKNOWLEDGMENTS

I would like to thank my sister Tessa and my brother Kits for their tremendous help and valuable support whilst I was writing this memoir.

My thanks are also due to my brother-in-law David Montgomery for his kind words of encouragement, and to my husband Peter for his infinite patience.

I owe Margaret Forster a huge debt of gratitude for her generous advice and guidance, and a big thank you to her husband Hunter Davies for introducing me to Bill Campbell of Mainstream Publishing.

Jim Matthews of Fowey, Cornwall, has done an excellent job in photographing the many tiny black and white snapshots, for which I am extremely grateful.

Finally, a salute to my two Burmese cats, Jakie and Astor, for their constant attention to the tap of the typewriter.

Daphne du Maurier

INTRODUCTION

I dream often that my mother is still alive. I suppose the unconscious mind is not yet reconciled to the fact that she is dead. In my dreams I see her as she was, a long time ago, before the start of the illness and depression that were to mar the last years of her life.

Sometimes in my dreams I am a child again, and we are all at Menabilly; Tessa is there and Kits and occasionally my father. We laugh, my mother is smiling and the sun is always shining.

On waking from these dreams I feel cheated; where have we all gone to, those happy, youthful beings? For in reality I am now middle aged and my mother is dead. I lie wakeful in the darkness and I think of Cornwall and how we came to be there in the first place. I realise how much we owe our du Maurier grandparents, for it was they who bought the holiday house, Ferryside, over at Bodinnick by Fowey. There my mother started to put down 'roots', to find the peace and freedom she had been seeking and have the inspiration to develop her fertile imagination as a writer.

In Cornwall she was to make her home, become at one with the beautiful rugged countryside and give to us a sense of belonging. She fell in love with a decaying old house called Menabilly and, with strength and determination, took a long lease upon the place, restoring it to its former glory. She gave Tessa, Kits and me a magical environment in which to grow up. It was a lovely haven for my father on his return from the stresses of the Second World War, and, in time, a retreat from the strain of London life.

My father came to Fowey for the first time after reading my mother's first novel, *The Loving Spirit*. He fell in love with both the author and Cornwall. The deep affection and respect they had for each other was to remain with them all their married life. They shared a love of the sea and boats and sailing, and they explored the countryside and got to know its history both past and present.

There were times when my parents had to be apart, and I missed the paternal contact during the war years, we all did, and those vital times are lost, forever elusive. My mother had to take on the role of both parents and we responded and gave her all our love and support. She became the very centre of our world.

My parents came from very different backgrounds though they shared one thing in common: they both had fathers with extremely powerful personalities who dominated their wives and children.

My father, Frederick Arthur Montague, was born on 20 December 1896, the only son of Colonel Frederick and Anne Browning. Colonel Freddie, a scion of an old Suffolk family, had been a keen sportsman, twice winning the Doubles Rackets Championships. He had been chairman of a small family wine shipping company which largely imported Hennessy brandy. As a friend of D'Oyly Carte, the hotelier and impresario who had built the Savoy Theatre, he had become a founding director of the Savoy Hotel. A man of unusual charm, with many friends, he became a very senior member of the British Intelligence Service during the 1914–18 War, for which he was awarded the CBE.

My father adored his pretty mother. She was a sweet, gentle person, though sometimes given to quick outbursts of temper when having to deal with the wilful behaviour of her son 'Tommy' as a small boy. Colonel Freddie was forced to send his son to prep school at an early age because of his unruly conduct – smashing all the glass in the greenhouses was a favourite occupation, as well as stoning the gardeners. His elder sister, Grace, suffered greatly from his bullying ways, and he would tear out her hair until she begged for mercy.

The prep school, West Downs at Winchester, proved a good choice and my father much enjoyed his time there. He remained in awe of the school's very austere headmaster all his life, often quoting from him, and he kept a photograph of the man in his bible. At Eton my father excelled as an athlete. In later life he won the High Hurdle Championship for England three seasons in succession and went on to represent Britain in the bob-sleigh team in the 1928 Olympics.

After going to Sandhurst he was commissioned into the Grenadier Guards, and in 1915 fought in France. He was awarded the DSO and French Croix de Guerre before his twentieth birthday. In 1924 he was made Adjutant of RMA Sandhurst, and it was while he was there that he earned the reputation as the best turned-out officer in the army, and was known for his strict discipline. It was my father who started the tradition of riding a horse up the steps of Old College after the Passing-out Parade. Apparently, the young cadets did such a bad rehearsal parade that my father cantered his grey horse, Spook, up the steps and into the building, and ordered them to come back and do the parade again.

In October 1929, Colonel Freddie died. He was only fifty-seven. His death was due to cirrhosis of the liver and worry over the great stock-market crash. He left his family almost penniless. This lack of personal funds was to dog my father all his life. He never had anything beyond his army pay, a fact brought home to him early in his career when he became unofficially engaged. One day, on going into the officers' mess, he noticed all his friends looking uneasy. He soon learned that his bride-to-be had become betrothed to one of his fellow officers, and his friends were trying to hide the news from him. He at once sent a telegram to the lady, saying, 'Please let me be the first to congratulate you. I wish you every happiness for the future'. It later transpired that she could not face married life on my father's slender means.

My mother was born, on 13 May 1907, into an artistic and talented family. Her grandfather, George du Maurier, had been the famous *Punch* cartoonist and writer, and Gerald, her father, one of the leading actor-managers of his day. The family had lived in a large house called Cannon Hall in Hampstead, and my mother and her two sisters, Angela and Jeanne, received private education at home with a governess. Early in life, my mother had shown promise as a writer, and was much encouraged by her adoring father.

The house was always filled with well-known folk from the world of the theatre and literature. The three girls enjoyed mixing with a wide variety of friends. My mother, who liked travelling, was given the opportunity to do so after spending some time in a small finishing-school in Paris.

She would tell us years later of the first time she stayed at Ferryside and of the visits to Cornwall. She would enthuse about her long, rambling walks along the cliffs, and of the first time she saw our beloved Menabilly with its ivy-clad walls. She had peered through broken shutters at gloomy ancestral portraits in dusty frames. We would shiver with delight as she recalled for us the sound of the owls hooting in the depth of the woods as dusk fell upon the darkening house.

The Menabilly we knew was bright and cheerful, the windows flung open wide to let the sun in. Tessa and I had once been taken to see the house in its neglected state before we had thought of living there, and briefly we had felt a moment of disquiet at the empty house, but the feeling had been quickly forgotten. I came to love the house and it was such a sadness the day I drove away through the park gates for the last time. I felt quite numb and I never did question my mother about the awful trauma it must have been for her. It went too deep, like a dreadful wound, and only time was able to heal such a hurt.

There were times when my mother was busy with her writing that I felt we were intruding on her life, the days when she would sit tap-tapping on the typewriter in her hut at the end of the lawn. She would be in a world of her own where we were not welcome. Her need for space, for freedom, was greater than her need for us. We would lose sight of her, she would become that far-off figure in a 'never never land', out of reach. She lived in distant times and places, peopled by the characters in her books, and they were beyond our childish comprehension.

My father would shrug his shoulders and sigh, and he would remark to us, 'Your mother lives in a dream' – and we would wait, biding our time until that magic moment when suddenly she was with us once more, the faraway look gone, her lovely face alive with joy and laughter, and we would all forget in a trice that feeling of abandonment and rejection. Life would resume once more its hazy, lazy days of childhood.

CHAPTER ONE

Rebecca and I were conceived about the same time in 1936, but whereas the novel was very much planned and thought-out, I was unquestionably a mistake. At the time my parents were stationed out in Egypt; my father, a colonel, was in command of the Second Battalion Grenadier Guards in Alexandria.

My mother had grown tired of the life out there; she hated the heat and the endless cocktail and dinner parties that took up so much of her time at Mustapha Barracks. She yearned for England and her beloved Cornwall, for the soft rain and green countryside. Ideas for a new book crowded into her mind and whenever she could she would lie in the shade of the garden of their rented house, jotting down thoughts in a small black notebook. She longed for the salt sea breezes to cool her, for the sticky, damp heat to lessen; and in her mind's eye she saw a large grey manor-house, its magnificent gardens stretching down to the craggy Cornish coast, a beautiful woman with a cloud of dark hair, and a handsome, brooding man, a shy young girl

. . . My mother craved the time and energy to write it all down, to be free of domestic and social duties.

When both parents discovered that another baby was due the following spring, they were surprised and shocked. They had not wanted another child so soon, for their three-year-old daughter, Tessa, was proving more than enough, in spite of having a full-time nanny. Morning-sickness added to my mother's misery and it was not until the late autumn that she felt well enough to travel with Nanny and Tessa back to England. They went to stay with Granny Browning, her mother-in-law, at her house, Rousham Rectory, at Steeple Aston in Oxfordshire. Anne Browning welcomed them all, happy to see her little grand-daughter, and they spent the winter there, moving to a rented flat in London in the spring to await the birth.

I was born on 2 April 1937, a great disappointment to both parents. My father, returning with his battalion to Wellington Barracks, came to see me a few days after I was born and, looking in the cradle, had muttered: 'Hmm, she's plain.' They had so wanted a boy, had chosen his name – Christian – and even painted the name on toy cupboards in anticipation. They found little cause for celebrating the arrival of another daughter. Tessa and I were dispatched as soon as possible with Nanny Egglesfield down to Rousham where we spent the next few months, my parents returning to Egypt until the late autumn.

When they came back, they visited us once or twice, but it was not until the following January that we were all together. I think it strange that they did not want to spend Christmas with their children; instead, they went to Cornwall and we made do in Nanny's little cottage in Bedfordshire. I have, of course, no memory of this separation, and I'm sure Nanny fulfilled her role as surrogate mother very well, giving us as much care and attention as she could; but I think it sad not to have had some sort of maternal bonding at such a young age.

My father's battalion had been sent to Pirbright Camp, and as a result he took an army hiring, a house called Greyfriars near Church Crooken in Hampshire, and we all moved there in the spring of 1938. It was a thatched house with small rooms and poky passages, but with a large, rambling garden bordered by a narrow wood. It was here among the trees, in a garden hut, that my mother wrote, finishing the novel *Rebecca* which she had started in the heat of Egypt. When it was published later that year it was an instant success, making her famous overnight.

I trespassed years later in the then overgrown gardens, and stared at the empty, forlorn house and tumbled-down hut, and tried to recapture those former years, seeing us all there. It was in that garden that I had learned to walk, and it was there that Tessa first realised she did not like me.

Tessa had her sixth birthday at Greyfriars, and she had been the apple of everybody's eye, much doted on by Nanny; but now Nanny had begun to lavish affection on the eighteen-month-old baby, and Tessa resented this bitterly. For her birthday she had been given a beautiful Shirley Temple doll by her godmother, Atalanta Arlen. The doll had a china face and real golden curls, and a pretty, frilly dress. Tessa adored the doll, playing endless games with it, pushing it about in a little pram. One day, sitting up in my pram, the doll was placed on the covers in front of me and, so I'm told, I snatched the doll and hurled it to the ground where it smashed into smithereens. Tessa was heartbroken. She told me a few years ago that that was the moment she took a positive dislike to me which lasted well into our teens, and it wasn't until she got engaged to be married that she suddenly found that she no longer hated and resented me. We are now close and the best of friends, but I often think both our lives would have been quite different if we had got on well as children.

We lived at Greyfriars while my father was at Pirbright, and on the outbreak of war in 1939 he was given command of the Small Arms School at Netheravon. But as there was no suitable house there, he was given the commandant's house at Hythe in Kent.

During this time we were often packed off with Nanny to Granny Browning in Oxfordshire or to Nanny's cottage. My mother would sometimes visit us at the latter, driven there by Johnson, my father's batman (known in the Brigade of Guards as a soldier servant). Tessa and I would stand at the end of the garden path by a small green gate, waiting for her to arrive. At the back of the cottage was a tiny garden with laden plum trees, and here we would sit, and Nanny and my mother would chatter away while Tessa and I would clamour for their attention. When the time came for my mother to leave we would set up a howl and cling to her skirts, pleading with her to stay. Once the car was out of sight Nanny would scold us: 'Poor Mummy doesn't like being made upset like that. She will think you don't like your Nanny,' and her small mouth would pucker and her eyes shine with unshed tears, far more upset than our mother ever was at leaving us.

We spent most of 1939 with Nanny, away from Hythe, my mother thinking it safer to keep us from the coast in case of invasion. In May 1940 my father was made a brigadier and given command of the 128th Infantry Brigade, a training formation, and his headquarters became a secret address up in Hertford-shire. We became homeless.

Johnson, our soldier servant, was a very resourceful man. He took it upon himself to try and find accommodation for his commanding officer's family. One day he called by chance at a house near Hitchin in Hertford-shire. Within a short space of time he had arranged with the owners to accept the entire family as paying guests. My mother did not even bother to vet the place before moving there in June 1940. She arrived on her own, expecting to stay only a week, and imagining to find a villa or shabby old parsonage. She was amazed to see an exquisite Lutyens house amid lovely spacious grounds, and she was welcomed by a charming, pretty, tall woman in her early forties, dressed in smart tweeds, who showed her to a luxurious suite of double bed-room, dressing-room and bathroom, the latest in modern plumbing.

Downstairs was a stunning white drawing-room with magnificent vases of trailing lilac and lupins. Our host-ess was kindness itself, making my mother feel relaxed and welcome, and our host was tall and dark, remind-ing her of a young Compton Mackenzie. He had what she later described as a hauntingly familiar face, as if she had known and seen him in other days and in different company.

We became happily billeted on the sweet couple; Christopher and Paddy Puxley had no children of their own, and they received us into their home with much warmth and friendship. They took great trouble in creating a nursery wing for us, much to Nanny's delight. This suite of rooms looked out over the stable-yard and garages. Tessa and I shared a bedroom with our nursery-maid, Prim, engaged to help Nanny with the more mundane chores of nursery life. We soon settled down to a contented and comfortable routine at Langley End. The war, by now into its second year, meant very little to us, and we were too young to realise how much it affected the grown-ups.

My father's brigade in the neighbourhood meant that he was able to get back to Langley End at night. He was having a frustrating time with his men, blocking up roads in the district and ruthlessly erecting pill-boxes in the gardens of infuriated old gentlemen. He had a theory at the time that anyone over the age of sixty ought to be shot, and most civilians either interned or deported!

My mother worried a great deal over her mother and two sisters living down at Fowey in Cornwall, for they were enduring constant air alarms. She had many offers from the United States and the Dominions to take us children for the duration of the war, but she was scared that something might happen and she would never see us again. A bomb landing in a nearby wood with a terrific bang nearly caused her to change her mind. And my father telling her that the British Army had about as much hope of beating the Germans as an indifferent club side tackling internationals at Twickenham left her feeling all too vulnerable. He had a poor opinion of present-day Englishmen and their leaders, believing the whole nation to be fundamentally inefficient and ill-disciplined.

Christopher Puxley, who was the same age as my father, had been invalided at some juncture and now farmed and organised the local Civil Defence. We were sometimes allowed to follow him about the farm and fields, and he would lift me up high on to the back of one of the cart-horses and I would sit surveying the world from this lofty viewpoint, protesting when put down on to the ground once more. Christopher's eyes would smile kindly, diverting my attention to something else.

Paddy Puxley was very involved with running the local branch of the Red Cross and WVS. One of her duties was to drive a mobile soup-kitchen and I would occasionally be allowed to accompany her, sitting up beside her in the front. We would drive slowly along to various villages where Paddy would administer to the needy. I became very attached to Paddy and followed her about like a dog whenever I could. After nursery breakfast I would slip away unnoticed and creep along the pale green carpet to Paddy's bedroom and into bed beside her while she ate her breakfast of toast and coffee. She would put golden farm butter on small bites for me and we would giggle quietly, knowing how cross Nanny would be. While she had her bath I sat at her dressing-table and played with her scent bottles and silver hair-brushes.

She would take the white cotton rags out of my hair and softly brush out the long curls. Nanny was proud of my ringlets but she pulled my hair when brushing whereas Paddy was gentle. We would then proceed down the wide front staircase, out of bounds to us children, and on down to the large kitchen to see Cook about the meals. Cook was stout with grey hair in a bun. She gave me titbits to eat. 'Don't you tell your Nanny you had that,' she would laugh, 'or she'll skin me alive.' The very thought of this fate befalling Cook made me rush from the place and sometimes I would hide the offerings just in case.

Upstairs in the study Christopher, smoking his pipe, sat reading the paper. We would stare at each other and his brown eyes would twinkle and I would lean on the arm of his chair, waving away the smoke from his pipe. I never spoke and nor did he, though sometimes he hummed a tune which he had been playing earlier on the piano. He played often and the sound would echo through the house, beautiful and sometimes sad, and if I were to catch him sitting at his piano, his face would seem withdrawn and he didn't smile, but his eyes would watch me carefully, and soon I would feel unsure and drift away back to Nanny and the comforts of the nursery.

Nanny took great pride and delight in our appearance. She spent hours smocking pretty dresses for us and knitting cardigans and jerseys. She would often dress us alike, which Tessa hated. She would beg Nanny to let her wear a different dress to mine, but Nanny was firm: 'You should be pleased to dress like your little sister.' And Tessa would scowl, making cross faces at me, and there we would be, even down to the same shoes.

Tessa was tall for her age, slim, with fair hair cut in a short pageboy style. She had started attending a small class of about six or seven children at a large house owned by a family called Brand. Every day she would be taken by Nanny or Prim to join this group with their governess, together with some American children. Once a week there was a dancing class and Nanny would take me along to watch. Pretty little girls in purple tunics and Alice bands hopped and skipped round a large room with a shiny parquet floor. One day Nanny said to Tessa, 'Come dance with your sister,' and Tessa, with a look of loathing, dragged me on to the slippery floor – whereupon I promptly wet my knickers and the floor to Tessa's utter shame and disgust. She refused ever to have me watch a class again, pleading with Nanny to banish me from her sight. Nanny agreed, feeling herself let down by her charge.

Each day after tea we were allowed downstairs to the drawing-room. Dressed in frilly dresses we played with special toys, jigsaws and such like kept in a drawer of Paddy's desk. This was about the only time we saw my mother. She had started work on a new novel about old Cornwall called *Frenchman's Creek* and was a very shadowy figure at this time in my life. Christopher would sit playing the piano softly in the background, my mother leaning over him to turn the pages of his music. We would become aware of the rippling sound of the piano keys and the faint whiff of his pipe and he would watch us, his dark eyes now smiling, and he and my mother would laugh at some secret joke in a world of their own. Paddy, sitting on the sofa, played with us, her sweet smile lighting up her pretty face. I would climb on her knee and hug her tightly while Tessa, aloof, would watch the grown-ups and make the odd sharp remark too mature for comfort. Paddy would try to include her more, but she would remain detached.

It seems my father was at Langley End whenever possible, but I do not recall him at all. At that time all over England there were alarms of enemy landings along the coast, so he was kept very busy. His head-quarters had now moved to spacious stables belonging to a family called Harrison.

CHAPTER TWO

In October 1940 we moved out of Langley End for my mother was by then seven months pregnant. She rented a house nearby called Cloud's Hill. It belonged to Lord Lloyd, Minister for the Colonies, and she found him an alarming old gentleman who spoke English with a French accent, for some unknown reason, being English to the hilt. His wife had been lady-in-waiting to Queen Alexandra, and offended my mother by locking away all her best china and glass. The Lloyds were due to take the house back in January 1941.

My mother's pregnancy this time was welcomed by both parents; it was thought time to have a final effort at producing the much wanted son, though the thought of having 'another lumping daughter' was daunting. Tessa, bright as a button, guessed that her mother was having a baby: 'It strikes me Mummy is going to have a baby sister for us – she is wearing those awful smocks again.'

Cloud's Hill was much smaller and darker than Langley End but it had a nice garden with a large lawn leading down to a ha-ha, beyond which lay wide open fields. The family, called Harrison, lived quite close by and consisted of a hearty hunting squire, his sparkling, pretty wife, and eight unmarried daughters who soon became known as the 'Brigade Butterflies'. My father was fascinated by them all, and twirled his moustache on every occasion that he found himself in their company. He became the life and soul of any social gathering, performing his Russian Cossack dances at which he was very proficient. My mother, now large with child, took a very dim view of this, feeling a dud, and had what she called 'a fit of sour grapes'.

The 'Butterflies' sometimes galloped their fancy hunters over the fields and up to the ha-ha, where they would strain their eyes for a glimpse of the 'dashing brigadier'. We thought their arrival great fun, and would feed their horses, stroking the soft noses which would be level with our own.

I came to dislike Cloud's Hill because of the witches which apparently lurked there, waiting to pounce. It was soon after we moved in that Tessa and I were playing outside by a stone statue of a man and his deerhound which stood on the gravel sweep in front of the house, when a laundry van drew up. Tessa pointed at the wicker baskets piled high in the back. 'Look at those,' she said. 'They are full of babies, witches' babies being delivered. That's how our baby sister will arrive, in one of those baskets.' She then pulled a horrible face, cackling in a frightening way. Scared, I ran to tell Prim who laughed loudly at my tale, but it was not long after this event that I was woken in the night by Tessa, and pulled protesting down the passage to our mother's bedroom. I saw her lying in the dim light. By the side of her bed was a basket and, horror of horrors, when Tessa pushed me forward, I saw that she had been right: there was a witch's baby, its face all wrinkly like a squashed doll, weird sounds coming from its mouth. I screamed and fled back to our room and lay terrified in bed, the sheets pulled up over my head.

Slowly, the awful image of my brother Christian faded from my mind to be replaced with curiosity. It was amazing to see the tiny, pink creature in his bath, splashing for all he was worth, held by my mother – for it was she who bathed him, not Nanny. She had waited seven years to read in *The Times*, 'To Mrs Browning – a son.' She adored Christian Frederick du Maurier Browning from the first minute she clapped eyes on him, hugging and kissing him in a way which made Tessa and I stare in astonishment, for we had never received such treatment. We would watch him lying gurgling in her arms, her face buried in his tiny neck, and we would slip from the room, uncomfortable, knowing we were not wanted there.

My father was able to see Christian before going with his troops to a new, secret area on the south coast. The war had come between him and his son and heir, but his feelings of relief and delight in at last having a boy did not match the overwhelming joy of my mother.

At his christening Christian yelled at the top of his lungs. The noise was dreadful and made his father mutter 'Bloody hell' once or twice. Granny Browning, holding tightly to my hand, whispered to me that it was a good thing to cry at this time. 'The Devil flies out of him, you see,' she said, bending her gentle, kind face down to me. 'His little soul will now be pure and true, he will be trailing clouds of glory.' I remember, once outside the church, glancing anxiously up at the sky and wondering what she could have meant. For some reason after Christian's birth I used to wet

my bed, causing Nanny to rub my face in the soiled
sheets.

We spent the Christmas of 1940 at Cloud's Hill and
then, because the Lloyds wanted their house back,
found ourselves homeless. There were no houses to
rent in the district, so once more the Puxleys came to
our rescue. It was all the more noble of them as they
had taken in refugees and we now numbered thirteen
in all at Langley End. Perhaps the number was unlucky
for we had no sooner settled down when a number of
mishaps befell us. Nanny had a sort of nervous collapse
and was ordered to bed by the doctor for a complete
rest. My mother had to lay aside her writing and take
charge of Christian who she claimed had the temperament of an angel as he only smiled happily through her
bungling management. And then, just as Nanny was
getting better, Tessa went down with measles caught at
a party a few weeks before.

The party had been quite an event in our lives. It was
the first children's party we had ever been to. Scarlet in
the face, ringlets atremble, and dressed to kill in fluffy
frocks, we had set off escorted by Prim. The party was
in a very grand house, and after an enormous tea
served by a mass of white-starched nannies we were
made to play games. I remember sitting next to a small
freckle-faced boy who refused to pass the parcel to me
in the game, so I took off my red bar shoe and whacked
him several times over the head. His screams of rage
and pain brought eagle-eyed nurses sprinting from all
corners of the room, whereupon I slunk away and hid
behind a giant sofa. From there I watched at a safe
distance while Oranges and Lemons and Nuts in May

were played. The party coincided with a rare visit from my father who had volunteered to collect us. Years later he was to tell of how, surveying the room teeming with children, he had turned to the hostess and asked, 'Who is that pretty little girl over there?' Only to be told 'That, Tommy, is your daughter, Flavia.'

Tessa was very poorly with the measles and was moved into my mother's room and Nanny, still groggy, was handed back Kits. It was a matter of weeks before I too fell ill and replaced Tessa in my mother's room. It was really the first time I had had any close contact with her and remember well the half darkened room and her bending over me with sips of water. As I recovered my mother would bring her typewriter and sit by my bed, the clack clack clack making a comforting noise, and now and then she would look at me in an absent way and smile, and I would snuggle in the bed happily.

In April I celebrated my fourth birthday. On the morning I rushed into Paddy's bedroom where she was sitting up, breakfast tray before her. I climbed in beside her and we played hunt the present. Thoughts of a teddy or a horse on wheels filled my head.

'Flavia,' she said, 'I have a very special present for you,' and from under her pillow she drew a slim, brightly coloured package.

Flushed with excitement, I tore off the paper and saw a white satin box. She took it from me and opened it. 'Look. This is a fan which I have had since I was a child like you and I have always loved it. I would like you to have it now.' Her sweet face beamed down at me and she spread out the white fan. There were ladies in long pink dresses reclining under green trees painted on it, and soft white lace at the edges. Paddy waved it gently to and fro and I felt a light draught on my cheeks. I hope I thanked her for I remember grabbing the fan and rushing from the room, overcome with disappointment. My mother gave me all the Beatrix Potter books in a little blue case and, although I had not been taught my letters, I pored over the pictures and pestered poor Paddy to read to me.

Playing in the garden a few days later I came across the fan, wet, torn and bedraggled. I must have left it out and the rain had washed away the ladies' bright pink dresses, and the lace had come apart. I stood holding the damp spent thing, fearful Paddy would find me. I took it to Nanny, crying, and she did her best to clean it up, but it remained a shadow of its former self.

Christian was now at the crawling stage and we girls adored him. He was never still for a moment. My mother worshipped him, taking charge whenever possible. Nanny went to her cottage to convalesce and Tessa and I were left in the hands of Prim.

Prim was large and jolly and rather clumsy. Our nursery meals had to be carried upstairs from the kitchen and Prim would stagger up the narrow back way and barge into the room. More than once the overladen tray slipped from her hands and crashed to the floor, stews and fruit salads flying in all directions. We would scamper about in delight, helping to mop up the mess, and then I'd tear down to the kitchen and beg for more food. Cook, cross with endless dishing up, would sigh and chase me away, grumbling to the housemaids. Tessa and I would go and sit by the green baize door waiting for leftovers from the dining-room and hoping for a glimpse of my mother before she settled to her writing. More often than not we were shooed away and the door firmly shut in our faces.

That spring my mother suddenly became ill with a

chill on the lung which quickly turned into septic pneumonia. She was lucky enough to be given the new drug, M & B, and for days she lay in bed, wretched and weak. When she had recovered she felt tired and listless and would lie on the sofa in the drawing-room while Christopher played the piano to her.

Nanny had remained at her cottage and so, with Prim minding Christian, Tessa and I went to Granny at Rousham. We had not been there long when we both got whooping cough and were so unwell that Nanny was sent for. The wracking cough and endless sickness left Tessa and me thin and fractious. We stayed on at Rousham to lighten the load at Langley End and to give my mother a chance to get on with *Frenchman's Creek*, a story which she described as a Romance with a big R. She hoped it would help her readers forget the war.

My father was now commanding the 24th Guards Brigade 'somewhere in England' and only got back occasionally for a night.

We enjoyed the summer months with the Puxleys. We were all fit and well again and Christian, who had escaped the bugs, was in tearing spirits. He now came down to the drawing-room with us after tea and would make a beeline for a large red tin in the corner of the room which was full of sweets sent from America. He would keep us in fits of laughter trying to dance as he had seen my father do his Cossack act. He would put his arms above his head, his little legs going in all directions, and shouting at the top of his voice. He had great charm and knew when he was being funny.

He would cough loudly if no one took any notice of him and then smile like a matinee idol. My mother would swoop upon him, catching him up in her arms, covering his face with kisses, and Tessa would nudge me and raise her eyebrows and we would for a second feel a moment of closeness in our longing to be treated in like manner, but it never happened.

My parents were able to snatch two weeks together at the end of the summer. They went to Fowey in Cornwall and stayed on the boat which they kept there. They were amazed how quiet and untroubled the place was; hardly more than a sprinkling of barbed wire on the quays and few naval ships.

At last *Frenchman's Creek* was finished and published, and Paddy and Christopher were given advance copies for my mother had dedicated the book to them. She said that the Frenchman was a mixture of my father and Christopher.

CHAPTER THREE

My mother's love of Cornwall and her great longing to live there finally persuaded her to move to the country. She rented a house for us all at Ready Money Cove near Fowey and we moved there in the summer of 1942. My father had now been chosen to head an experimental airborne formation and was kept extremely busy, moving all over the country, so he was very relieved and happy that we should at last be settled in a home of our own.

The house itself was called Ready Money, and was a bungalow-type building with a two-storeyed central part. It had been the stables for the large house standing on the top of some cliffs nearby called Pont Neptune. Ready Money was painted white with black window-sills, and a mass of pretty yellow roses straddled across the front part. At the back of the house was a large garden with wide lawns and a shrubbery with a little stream running through part of it. A tennis court was tucked behind a beech hedge at the far end. The main part of the house faced Ready Money Cove and the sea.

Huge iron bars about eighteen feet high, a fortification against enemy landing-craft, stretched along the beach, becoming partly submerged when the tide was in.

Inside the house was rather dark, except for the upstairs bedroom which my mother had. Directly below was the main living-room which was given over to us children as a play-room and family dining area, and this had a door leading to the garden. Tessa and I shared the only good-sized bedroom, with Nanny rather cramped in a small room next to the only bathroom. Christian had to make do with a cubbyhole of a room, just big enough for his cot. On the left-hand side of the house was a tiny kitchen and a narrow room that my mother turned into a study for herself and my father when he was at home. It was all rather a hugger-mugger set-up and we found it very constricting at first after the spacious rooms at Langley End.

I missed Paddy dreadfully. She had taken such trouble with me, had been so loving and kind. I fretted for weeks, also missing dear Prim who had to leave us for there was no room for her now. Many a tear was spilt over her departure.

Nanny suffered, feeling at times that everything was quite beyond her. But she had high hopes of my mother taking full charge of Christian. Here, though, she found a stumbling-block, for once more my mother had a book on the boil and this time it was proving to be quite a saga – 'could well be as long as *Gone with the Wind*', Nanny was told cheerfully. 'Copper-mines in 1825 Ireland!' It was Christopher Puxley who had been the inspiration behind the plot; he had owned a beautiful house in Ireland which had been burnt down in the 1920 Troubles.

Tessa had started going to day-school. St David's was along the Esplanade, about half a mile away, and looked out over Fowey harbour. She would walk there on her own in the mornings and Nanny would take Kits and me to meet her at lunchtime.

The Esplanade was a long road with houses on either side with lovely views over towards Polruan on the other side of Fowey harbour. A ferry ran back and forth and sometimes we would go and watch this if we had time to kill. On fine days we would rush back to Ready Money and make for the beach and the iron bars. The latter were a tremendous source of fun and daring. We had terrific games and adventures on them, egging each other on to climb ever higher, and then sitting down to watch the tide come in, creeping up, to catch our dangling feet, feeling a thrill as it splashed nearer and nearer.

Both Nanny and my mother strictly forbade us to clamber on the bars, but as the house was so close we could escape in no time, have a quick swing and race back before they were any the wiser. My mother had once heard tell of a woman called Mrs Brown. Dreadful things were always befalling this poor lady's children, so my mother would say, 'Now, look here, I feel like Mrs Brown, something awful will happen to you if you disobey.' 'Mrs Brown' became a catch-phrase for anything forbidden and dangerous. We had many such words in the family, code-words that only we knew. 'A hard chair' meant you were offended, 'wain' was embarrassed, 'honks' working class, and 'menacing' was said about someone wildly attractive. There were many more and it was possible to carry on a conversation about someone in their presence if you just called them 'Mrs Chichester' or Mr; they might even join in, not realising that they were being discussed. A handful of close friends were enlightened to 'words' and they would adopt them.

It was about this time that I remember my mother clearly for the first time. She appeared tall with broad shoulders, and her fair hair was lightly permed and almost shoulder-length. She had deep blue eyes which always seemed full of laughter. We adored her, always wanting to be with her. She was gentle and kind and though a little bored with us girls, idolising Christian, we forgave her this for it was a small price to pay for her company, for her to take an interest in our childish play. My mother never became cross or impatient with us, I never saw her lose her temper or get irritated as Nanny did on occasion. She was always cheerful and smiling with a great sense of humour. She had a feeling for fun and adventure as long as it was not harmful in any way.

Christian was getting on for eighteen months now, and was a divine-looking boy, chubby with white gold hair, blue eyes and a fierce temper when thwarted. Tessa and I were slightly jealous of him, but his wonderful cheerfulness of spirit made it impossible to bear a grudge for long. We would look on as my mother kissed and cuddled him, wishing that just once she might kiss or hug us but she never did. After a while we took it for granted that he should receive all the petting and so we would give him the odd kiss, more to please my mother than ourselves. He did look irresistible when all dressed up in his white sailor-suit.

We girls started to call him Kits, for he could not pronounce his own name, and he remains Kits to this day. At the same time we called my mother Bing after the bob-tailed sheepdog she had had as a young girl. We were a great family for nicknames: Kits and I called each other Beaver and today we are both known as Bee; my father became Moper, because he used to get so downcast about returning to London at the end of his weekends with us in Cornwall, he would sit and mope. Only Tessa has escaped.

Although we lived in close proximity, we saw little of Bing during the day because of her strict writing routine. We would hear the tap tap tapping of the typewriter from behind her closed door until lunchtime. Even Kits' bawls at being put down for his rest at midday did not stop the writing flow.

Nanny would busy herself about the house, closely followed by me if she had to tackle the awesome job of clearing the one and only bathroom of the hordes of black-beetles which infested the bath. In spite of all the domestic work, Nanny still found time to make our clothes. She spent hours at her sewing-machine and I would be detailed to look after Kits, a task I found most tedious. He was four years younger and I found him often fretful and whiny, difficult to keep amused for long. It was no good making a fuss, for Nanny would either smack me on the legs or get on such a 'hard chair' that I hadn't the heart to complain. I longed for Paddy and Prim to come to the rescue.

Some mornings Nanny would wake with one of her 'heads'. This was bad news, as she would lie prone in her dark, little room, moaning until Mrs Staton arrived. She was the good body who came to cook for us, and she usually did the shopping *en route*. She would bustle in and get Bing's breakfast, taking the tray up to her room, and most days help Nanny with our breakfast. Days like these always led to utter chaos. Tessa would grumble loudly that she had no clean clothes; Kits, standing in his cot, long after he should have been got up, would bellow, soaking wet, shaking and rattling the sides of his cot, so that poor Nanny, lying in some misery next door, would pray for peace and quiet and a cup of hot sweet tea; and I would be trying, with tears streaming down my face, to disentangle my hair from the white cotton rags Nanny had put there the night before.

Bing would be oblivious to all this upheaval, safely tucked away in her room, calmly eating her breakfast. She was the only one who could be guaranteed to be fed and watered. At last all would be quiet, Tessa packed off to school, Mrs Staton behind a closed kitchen door and me trying to keep Kits entertained until his midday rest. Then I would be off like a hare to the beach, having first made sure the typewriter was busy at work. Up on to the bars I would go, the rust marking my dress and skin. I remember once falling and soaking my clothes and creeping back to the gardens where I buried the wet dress and knickers in the shrubbery. For days I kept very quiet, behaving in a model way. The clothes were never missed.

After tea, if it was very wet or cold, Bing would read to us in her study. She told us all about King Arthur and the Round Table. I became enthralled with the story and pored over the pictures in the children's edition. There was one scene in particular that captured my imagination – that of King Arthur and a knight fighting on horseback, the King's sword buried deep in the stomach of the helpless knight as he was forced back along his horse's saddle, an agonised look on his face. He wore an orange tunic over his armour and I pestered Nanny to make me a replica garment; this she did, from an old petticoat. I wore it proudly over my clothes and, armed with a wooden sword, spent all my free time fighting imaginary knights in the shrubbery.

I became a target for Tessa's ridicule. On seeing me emerge from mortal combat, she would stand and point at me, laughing, 'What do you look like, you silly fool,' and I would flush and walk away, feeling somehow guilty of my Arthurian games. The animosity grew between us and at times she could not open her mouth without saying a derogatory remark. This became more apparent when it suddenly dawned on Bing that I ought to start school. I was now five and had never had a lesson in my life. Tessa declared at once that she refused to go to the same school as me. This proved impossible for there were no other suitable schools near by.

So the day came when I was due to go. I became quite excited by the thought and set off up the hill in a newly smocked dress, ringlets tightly curled. Tessa had been told to take my hand, but as soon as we were out of sight of Nanny she flung my hand away and darted off at a fine pace, her pigtails swinging, leaving me trailing after her. I ran fast to try and keep up, but she was soon well out of sight. I knew the way well so I didn't mind, but my long socks were forever coming down in spite of the string tied round to keep them up. Tessa strode into the entrance of the school, leaving me standing bewildered on the garden path.

There were lots of small girls rushing in and out and I followed them and hung about the hall wondering what to do. At last to my relief a mistress came and took my hand and led me into a big room full of desks and chairs. The whole school seemed to be at work in that one room. I glimpsed Tessa at the far end sitting bowed over her desk, her head bent over a book. She never looked in my direction, for which I was grateful for I was close to tears.

The mistress made a circle of chairs in a corner by the large window and about six little girls sat down with her in the middle. Cloth books were handed out to us. The mistress was very chirpy and merry, her hair in a floppy bun which kept slipping loose so that she was forever putting her hands up to her head to smooth and twist it. 'Now, dears,' she said, 'who can read out loud to us all?'

I wriggled with excitement, 'I can, I can,' I said, the book shaking in my hands. She beamed at me and we turned to page one. In silence I followed the words to the end of the page and grinned up at the teacher.

'Read it out loud, so that we can hear,' she said. I was stumped: no one had taught me my letters. I had never had any sort of lesson before, and I thought reading was merely following the lines of words to the end of each page; they had never conveyed anything to me. 'Well, that was a naughty little lie to tell, wasn't it, dear?' The mistress clucked her tongue in disapproval and the small faces of the other children turned to look at me. One tittered. I went scarlet, feeling shame and utter amazement. I was certain I could read.

The rest of the morning I sat silent and miserable, and could not drink the horrid, cold boiled milk at break. At the end of school Tessa raced home ahead of me and with glee told of my stupidity, having been informed of her little sister's idle boast.

Bing promptly put aside some time to try and teach me the alphabet. I filled pages with B, D, U and V. They looked alike to me. And the sounds of S and C, I couldn't tell the difference. To my utter despair and the mockery of my sister, I did not learn to read well until I was seven. Strangely enough, my Aunt Angela used to buttonhole me and say, 'Learnt to read yet?' This was usually asked within earshot of the family so that I could not fabricate. At last one day, looking at the pictures of poor Ginger collapsed between the shafts in *Black Beauty*, the words suddenly sprang alive and I could read. The sense of achievement was overwhelming and wonderful.

There were occasions when there was a brief truce between Tessa and me and we would play a game or two together. She even became quite keen on my beloved King Arthur. She would dress up as Morgan Le Faye – the picture in the book resembled her quite remarkably – and if I begged she would be the Black Knight and we would play in Bing's study after tea, sitting astride the arms of the sofa pretending they were horses. One day after a good fight, I, the slain knight, crashed to the floor and hit my head against the corner of a chair, cutting my forehead. Blood poured forth and so did my screams. Nanny rushed in from bathing Kits and slumped to the floor in a dead faint. Chaos reigned, Tessa crying, 'Do something, do something!', though Bing was more fussed that Kits would drown in his bath than that I would bleed to death in the study. Eventually a sweet old doctor called King came and put a couple of stitches in my head. He was kind and gentle and hummed quietly as he administered to me.

Sadly, my soldier father was an infrequent visitor to Ready Money. His rare appearances were unannounced, so coming back from an afternoon walk we would enter the house and smell the faint aroma of lavender cologne and Woodbines. Tessa would cry, 'Daddy is home!' and we would rush into the study, and sure enough there he would be sitting in an armchair. We would fling our arms around him, hugging him, and he, somewhat startled, would tell us to stand still so that he could look at us to see if we had grown since last we met. 'We have, we have!' we would shout and he would give us sips of his gin and lime.

When at last we were in bed my father would look in through the bedroom window and pretend to walk down imaginary steps. First he would appear very tall and then get smaller and smaller until he disappeared altogether. Then up he would pop again, a very surprised look on his face. We thought this hilarious and screamed with delight, and shouted for more. Nanny would come in, complaining that we were keeping Kits awake and that it would all end in tears. It did one night. For some unknown reason I put my tongue out at my father in a very rude manner. Quick as a flash he came and walloped my bottom to the surprise of us all. I yelled with pain and hurt pride and Tessa, full of shame for me, hid under the bedcovers and refused to speak to me till morning.

If my father was with us for any length of time, he would take us visiting the neighbours. Just up the hill from us lived Hilda Fox, grandmother of the future acting family, Edward and Willie and their brother Robert. Mrs Fox had a small white cottage opposite the imposing building, Pont Neptune. Her daughter Mary shared a small market-garden near Fowey with my Aunt Jeanne. Mrs Fox made us gingerbread men and we would sit munching these while she talked and laughed with my father. She was small and stout with snow-white hair and lovely brown eyes.

Further up the hill lived a lady called Mrs Merchie. We might call on her and she was jolly and rather skittish, with jet black hair and a lot of rouge upon her cheeks, and dark red lips. There was an upright piano in her living-room and I used to sit at this and strum away tunelessly until made to stop. Mrs Merchie had a lodger, a gentleman of indeterminate age, known as the Captain. He always dressed in seaman's clothes and smoked a large pipe with much huffing and puffing. My father thought he was a smuggler or gunrunner and he would sit talking to him while Mrs Merchie entertained us. Sitting on a bright chintz sofa she looked rather like a black shiny crow, her head on one side, dark eyes twinkling merrily. She spoke in a clipped, quick voice and talked of the time she had been an actress. She would encourage us in our childish exploits, dressing us up in her funny hats and shawls so we could play charades, and she would exclaim, 'My goodness, whatever next?' and call out to my father to look and he would wave a hand, smoke curling from his cigarette.

Walking through Fowey one day, my father told Tessa and me of the plans he had of building a yacht when the war ended. His great love was for boats and the sea. If he had not been colour-blind, he said, he would have gone into the navy. He did own a small motor-boat called *Ygdrasil*, on which he and my mother had gone on their honeymoon to the Helford river. The boat was now laid up at Hunkin's, a boatyard in Fowey.

We listened to his ideas, but we were more interested in the goings on of the American fleet in Fowey harbour, with amphibian craft toing and froing between the Town and Albert quays. At the mouth of Fowey harbour, on either side of the channel, stood two ruined castles. My father explained to us that an underwater chain stretched between the two, which could be raised and lowered in defence against German submarines. The harbour now was overflowing with American ships and a French fishing fleet from Brittany, which had been trapped at the outbreak of war. These brightly coloured vessels would visit all the Cornish harbours in turn, and were greatly welcomed by the locals who were always thrilled when they happened to be in Fowey.

On the cliffs and in the woods to the west of Ready Money was a huge American army camp, swarming with GIs, which was firmly out of bounds to all civilians. Occasionally GIs would wander down to swim and lark about on the beach. Tessa and I would dart out of our gate and accost them, shrieking, 'Have you any gum, chum?'

The American officers had taken over the Rock Hotel as an officers' mess. This building, a smart, pale orange-coloured place, was next to St David's school, and rumour had it that they wanted the school in order to billet their soldiers. It was a great worry to local parents.

We were playing on the beach one day when we heard the sound of a low aircraft, and suddenly a plane came whining over our heads, great flames shooting out of it, the high pitch of its engines quite fearful. It came so low that we had a glimpse of the pilot before he became engulfed in smoke. The plane crashed head-long into the sea, just beyond the cove. Nanny, who happened to be with us, said, 'Good riddance to those nasty Germans,' but it shook Tessa and me dreadfully.

It was at this time that I had the notion that if only I could get to Germany and see Hitler, explain to him about our father being away from us and so many people being sad and unhappy, that he, Hitler, would stop the war. I was convinced that he would listen to me. But when I told Tessa of my idea she poured scorn on the plan: 'Stupid fool – as if anyone would take notice of a squirt like you.'

We had no friends of our own age until we broke the ice with another family, the Beddingfields, who lived about a hundred yards away at Ready Money Cove. My mother was no help at all, for she didn't want anyone to intrude on her writing and so never encour-aged even an acquaintance, though was forced to do Civil Defence with one or two neighbours. Elizabeth Beddingfield was my age, with pale, sandy hair worn in an Alice band. We became firm friends, the one and only I ever really had until I went to boarding-school at thirteen. Elizabeth had an elder brother, Hugh, who was a chorister at King's School, Canterbury. Once, when I was struggling alone on the iron bars, I saw him way above me walking easily on the very top section, singing in a wonderful treble voice, 'Oh, for the wings of a dove,' the sun shining on his auburn hair, completely fearless. Tessa and he became friends and the four of us spent a lot of time in each other's houses and in our back garden, jumping the tennis net, seeing who could manage the highest.

CHAPTER FOUR

Bing's mother, Lady du Maurier, lived over at Bodin-nick across the water from Fowey, and we would sometimes be taken to visit her for tea or, as a big treat, lunch. We would set off in good time, my mother wheeling Kits in his push-chair, Tessa and I neatly dressed in matching dresses made with loving care by Nanny. The latter would take advantage of our departure to have her hair permed: 'I want it done just like your Mummy's,' she would say, and indeed she tried, much to Bing's irritation.

On our way through Fowey we would sometimes stop at a lovely house called The Haven. It stood in pretty gardens up above the harbour with views out towards Polruan. Lady Quiller-Couch lived here, the wife of the great Cornish writer, Arthur Quiller-Couch, who was known in literary circles as 'Q'. He had met Bing when she had first come to live at Ferryside on her own in her early twenties, and had given her much good advice and encouragement when she was writing her first novel and poems.

Lady Q was a dear little person, dressed in lilac silk to her ankles, with fine lace about her throat, grey hair in a neat bun. Her daughter Foy was a great friend of Bing's. She kept a large market-garden on the Polruan-Bodinnick side of the harbour, and was dark, rather gypsy-like in appearance, often dressed in exotic-coloured stockings and an old-fashioned sun-bonnet in summer. I was drawn to her because she kept a pony and jingle which we ventured out in, a great event much looked forward to.

My grandmother often stood looking over the wall, watching for our arrival. Ferryside was just above the ferry slipway and was surrounded by a high stone wall at that point. The house had originally been a boat-house and was hewn out of the rock walls on one side with the water of the harbour lapping at the garden walls on the other. Painted pale yellow, with green windows and shutters, it had a mass of Virginia creeper growing up the outside. Under Gran's bedroom window hung a large, brightly painted figurehead of a lady who faced out towards the mouth of the harbour and the open sea. She was called Jane Slade after a woman of that name whose family had been boat-builders over at Polruan.

We would enter the big green gates and walk along the gravel path which skirted the wide lawn. A pretty stone well stood in the centre, pink geraniums struggling up its rustic bars. Thick clumps of hydrangeas grew near the thick wooden front door with its carved face, like the portcullis of a castle.

Inside Ferryside the flagstone hall led into the long drawing-room. On the left the wall was rough slate and rock, hewn out of the side of the hill, and on the right windows gave a wonderful view over the harbour. There were big chintz sofas and chairs, a long, highly polished refectory table piled high with books and magazines, and a large piano at the far end of the room which my Aunt Jeanne played. On the wall behind the piano was a portrait of my grandfather, the actor Gerald du Maurier, cigarette in hand as usual. It was a lovely room and always smelt faintly of Gran's special scent, Narcissus Noir, by Carron. We loved the house and enjoyed roaming all over it.

We all adored Gran, as we called my grandmother. 'Darlings!' she would greet us and sweep us into her arms with delight. Gran was very pretty, with dark auburn hair tightly curled in a sausage roll at the back, bright hazel eyes, lovely skin and a rather full figure. As a young actress she had been very beautiful and slim but had soon given up the stage to look after her husband and their growing family.

Our two aunts, Angela and Jeanne, lived with their mother at Ferryside. They were both land-girls, a job which poor Angela simply detested. She was the eldest of the du Maurier girls, Bing being in the middle. She was dark and not very tall with a great sense of fun and a delightful giggle. We enjoyed her company very much for she was always easy and relaxed. We were not so sure of Jeanne, for although very fair and pretty she seemed rather remote and shy, inclined to be sharp and impatient with us. She was a very good artist and her bedroom often smelt deliciously of turps, linseed oil and paint. They all adored Pekinese dogs, and there were usually at least three or four of these creatures running about, snapping at our ankles. We never took to these animals and the feeling was clearly mutual.

Up in the garden behind the house on a level with Gran's bedroom and balcony was a narrow strip of lawn with spectacular views across the harbour to the sea. On the lawn stood Gran's hammock, covered in flowered linen material and fat, comfy cushions. Tessa and I would make a beeline for this and throw ourselves on to it and swing back and forth, keeping our feet well clear of any lurking dogs.

It was such a treat to stay to lunch, Gran's food being always so much nicer than ours at home. She made the most delicious pastry which we wolfed. After the pudding was cleared by Ethel, the maid, Gran would make a great to-do with making the coffee in a glass cona which boiled water above a flame. One day I remember the whole thing blew up, sending water, glass and coffee in all directions. Gran lost her temper and shouted at poor Ethel, giving her an awful ticking off and blaming her for the mishap. Tessa and I got a fit of helpless giggles and were sent from the room, closely followed by Bing and Kits, tears of laughter pouring down my mother's cheeks.

We spent Christmas day at Ferryside that year, fighting our way across the ferry in teeming rain. Gran was able to get hold of a turkey and some crackers. Tessa and Bing had returned from church outraged that there had been no attempt at decorating the church: 'Not one miserly sprig of holly, and such a gloomy service – and they complain the churches are not filled and wonder why.'

My father had not been able to get leave to visit us, and in the New Year he was made a major-general, commanding the 1st Airborne Division. We were all very proud of him and when Granny Browning came to stay she started us on a nightly prayer régime which we kept up throughout the war, praying for our father's safe return.

Bing spent much of the early spring of 1943 correcting the proofs of her Irish novel, *Hungry Hill*, and on 5 May it was published. She grumbled about the poor-quality paper used, thinking it made the book look cheap and nasty. She was furious that the Government made her pay so much in tax on the film rights of *Frenchman's Creek* which she had recently sold: 'I have given the Government enough money for them to build another Lancaster bomber.'

When my father crashed in a glider, badly hurting his knee, Bing rushed up to Netheravon to his bedside and brought him back down to us for two weeks' leave. He lay in bed a good deal, rather grumpy, with a painful clot on the knee, and when he recovered he had to fly to North Africa to meet General Alexander, which made my mother very 'Mrs Brown'.

The Americans finally took over our school building, and it was forced to close down. Bing had to set about trying to teach us herself. Her whole routine changed and she turned her study into a temporary schoolroom. She was distressed at how little we knew and complained to Nanny, 'I can't imagine what they have done at St David's. Tess still doesn't know her three times table and Flave is very hazy on the wretched alphabet.'

She launched us into the most interesting of lessons, mostly taken from the *Children's Encyclopaedia*. We learned the wonderful tale of the Black Prince winning his spurs, the story of Joan of Arc, the Black Death with cries of 'Bring out your dead!'. Tessa and I walked round the houses in Ready Money Cove calling this out, pushing an old wheelbarrow draped in a piece of black cloth. We did Chaucer – *The Canterbury Tales* – and learnt of lepers ringing their bells. This sent Nanny wild with annoyance for I would then wake up screaming with nightmares. 'I wish Mummy would not tell you these horrid things, it's not fit for young ears,' she said. We took the world in one fell swoop in our geography lessons. We could not get enough of the dizzy, bewildering mixture Bing taught us, and even clamoured for more. This was how I had imagined school would be.

There were days when Bing had to be free of us. Then we would be sent over to Gran at Ferryside or to see Mrs Hancock who had been our cook at Greyfriars and was a native of Fowey. She was retired and lived with her sister Mrs Hunkin and husband George over Bodinnick way, up the hill on the road to Looe. Their house looked over to Fowey china clay jetties at the mouth of the River Fowey. George Hunkin was a boat-builder and his yard was below the house at the water's edge. Tessa and I enjoyed our visits for Mrs Hunkin made the most delicious Cornish pasties, and instead of the usual meat filled them with crunchy bacon. After lunch we would play in the garden until it was time for tea: home-made splits with yellow clotted cream and strawberry jam, dark saffron buns and sometimes a fresh fruit jelly. We would stuff ourselves, chatting away to Hanks, as we called Mrs Hancock, sometimes getting a fit of the giggles for no real reason. Then off down to Ferryside to meet Aunt Angela who was to take us back, walking through Fowey to Ready Money. This was usually fun for she knew so many people, and we would stop and talk and hover about, hoping to speak to American officers and perhaps be given some chewing-gum.

At the Fowey hotel there lived a rather sad but very elegant lady, tall and thin with very peroxide hair. She would sit on the terrace on fine evenings and smile down at us as we went by. She was always dressed in pink and blue and rather ridiculous sun-bonnets. Bing was much intrigued by her and used to say that she cried out to be in some strange story or other, and would make up adventures about her to our delight.

One spring day in 1943, Bing and Aunt Angela took Tessa and me on an outing to visit a house which my mother had fallen in love with many years before when she was a girl, living at Ferryside. It was this house that she had in mind when writing about Manderley in her novel, *Rebecca*.

We walked from Ready Money along the road until we came to two large wrought-iron gates by a small lodge. We pushed the rusted gates open and started walking for what seemed like miles along a narrow overgrown path that my mother said had once been a wide gravel drive. In places the path would for no reason broaden out under tall, beautiful beech trees which stretched overhead like the vast ceiling of some cathedral. Dense laurel and sweeping branches of scarlet rhododendron hampered our way, causing us to break off thick stems in order to get past. At last we turned left off the path and wound up through woods, dark and cool, the only sound that of our feet shuffling through the carpet of dead leaves and the soft call of the wood-pigeons overhead. Seeing strong sunlight ahead, Tessa and I ran the last bit and burst out of the trees on to a gravel path and there before us stood a large, grey house. We moved forward on to a lawn, the grass as high as our waists.

We followed Bing along the side of the building, the path overgrown with weeds, and as we neared the front we saw that it was completely covered in ivy, like a dark, green shroud, no windows visible. We stood staring at this extraordinary sight, and we became aware of a deep silence. We crept nearer, hardly daring to breathe, afraid of disturbing the entombed house.

We gently tried to part the ivy leaves from a peeling window frame and managed to peep inside the dirty pane, glimpsing rotting floorboards partly covered in fallen plaster, limp, torn wallpaper with a faded rose pattern hanging like a torn sheet from damp-streaked walls. We turned away, glad to be in the sun once more. We ate our picnic lunch sitting on the long grass, our eyes never straying long from the ivy walls.

I tried to imagine the house's former glory, for Bing told us that it belonged to a Dr Rashleigh, that it had been in that family since the seventeenth century, was entailed and could only go to male heirs. But Dr Rashleigh's second wife had not cared for the house, had found it too big and had not liked the atmosphere.

'Menabilly has been empty now for twenty years,' Bing continued, for that was the name of the house. She got to her feet and she went and put her hands out and buried them in the ivy, leaning her cheek against it, kissing the house. When she came back towards us her face was slightly flushed, her blue eyes very bright, almost dancing with some secret joy.

Tess and I wandered off across the lawn away from the grown-ups and we heard their voices raised, a hoot of laughter from Angela and her shout of protest: 'You are mad, you can't,' and we wondered what she meant and why they suddenly seemed so heated in their conversation.

At the end of the lawn we could see the sea in the far distance, blue with a hard line on the horizon. We turned and came back, the house looming very large as we advanced, the sun shining fully on the green mass. Tessa shivered slightly. 'Gloomy old place,' she said. 'I'm bored, wish we could go home,' and she delved into the picnic bag looking for leftovers.

We did not talk much on our return journey and I was very tired when we reached home. Nanny had gone away for a short holiday to get over the removal of several teeth and Mrs Hancock had come from

Bodinnick to cook and look after us. We sat with Hanks, telling her of our adventure.

A week later, when Nanny returned, she and Bing began to behave in a very odd way. They would remain in the study for ages, the door shut, and I would hear voices raised in argument. A strange man in a dark suit called often, bundles of papers under his arm, and there was more loud talk. Then Nanny would appear at meal-times grim-faced, and she and Bing and Hanks would whisper if we came upon them suddenly. It was all very strange. One day Bing and Nanny went out early in the morning and did not return until dark. This became their routine for weeks: off they would go, chatting and laughing, driven by kind friends who could spare the time and petrol, and armed with buckets and brooms and piles of dusters and rags.

We were mystified and not a little cross and anxious, for they refused to say where they were going. In the middle of all this Mrs Staton had left us, retired to some cottage, so Hanks was now full-time, cooking, cleaning and taking care of us children. Tessa and I played her up, forever going off to the iron bars, united in our sudden insecurity, coming back with wet clothes from too daring games in the sea. Tessa ate some flowers from a large rhododendron bush growing in the garden and came out in terrible spots, like some dreadful plague. She was very ill and the doctor had to be called, which sent Bing into a great state of 'Mrs Brown'. She came into our bedroom, her lovely face white and troubled.

'Look, my darlings, I know this is a muddling time for you, but please be good and behave and do what poor Hanks tells you. I have such a lovely surprise for you, something so wonderful and so exciting, but you must wait, wait and see.' She had smiled, her face full of light, and in her eyes a look that made us sit up in great anticipation.

'Tell us, tell us,' we begged, but she had got up and left us and we whispered long into the evening, trying to guess what Bing had in store for us.

CHAPTER FIVE

In early December 1943 we all went down with a fearful bout of flu. Bing and Nanny struggled out of their sick-beds to continue their strange visits. At last one day they arrived back tired, but with a look of triumph on their worn faces.

We children had been allowed out of bed for tea and were sitting by the study fire making toast with Hanks. My mother sipped her hot tea and said: 'Soon we shall be leaving here and going to live in our new home.' We stared. What did she mean? We liked our house, this was home. 'Yes, we are going to live in Menabilly and you will have a lovely big garden to play in.' We could not take in what she was saying. The idea of going to live in that huge, gloomy house covered in ivy was daunting. We were full of questions: whatever would Daddy think, had he seen it? But my mother looked so happy, smiling and chatting, that we soon caught her mood and grew excited, wanting to go there that very moment.

Two weeks later we arrived by hired car at the park

gates of Menabilly. A large sign said 'PRIVATE' and two little children ran out of the lodge and stared at us in wonder before pushing the gates open. We sped down across the park, gravel spurting up against the doors, and we pressed our noses to the cold window panes and gazed out at the many fine trees and at the red Devon cows cropping the winter grass. Then we were at another pair of gates, smaller than the last and covered in rust. Nanny got out and opened them and we left her as the car moved up a short hill bordered on either side by dark laurel bushes. Then we were out in the bright sun, drawing up on the white gravel sweep before the open front door.

Bing stood there smiling, her hands in the pockets of her blue cords, a slim, boyish figure. We scrambled out at her feet and she cried, 'Welcome to Mena!'

Tessa and I stared up at the windows. The ivy had gone and the white painted frames sparkled in the light. We followed Bing into a hall and I was surprised how bright it was with cheerful rugs on the floor. Bing took us into a room, the very one we had glimpsed months ago with the rotten floor and fallen ceiling. Its windows looked out across the lawn to the sea and its walls were now restored and covered in a pretty flowered paper which matched the sofa and chairs. A warm carpet covered the floor and a rocking horse stood prancing, his flared nostrils reflecting the red glare from the fire banked up in the grate.

We jumped with joy at the sight of our new nursery. Eager to see more we ran into the room on the right of the hall. This was a library, with panelled walls and books, a baby grand piano and hunting prints on the walls. An alcove large enough to use for dining was at the end of the room and here the floor was uncarpeted, brightly polished. A door there led to another smaller hall with a stable-type door to the side lawns, and on the left was a large staircase with walls of a powerful crimson on which hung an enormous picture of the du Maurier girls when young.

We bounded up these stairs which branched off to right and left and explored my parents' bedrooms and dressing-room and tore along the wide red-carpeted passage past the only bathroom and upstairs lavatory. We stood confronted by large white doors, locked and bolted against our pounding. We were told never to venture through these doors, for beyond lay the nineteenth-century addition to the house, a vast three-storey building, never really lived in and now falling into decay, with dry-rot taking its toll. It was strictly 'Mrs Brown' area, off limits to us. Back along the passage we found our own quarters, a lovely spacious room, directly above our nursery, and with splendid views. Green lino and gay rugs covered the floor. Three beds stood in a row, for we were all to share the room. This caused tears with Tessa, who stamped her foot, demanding her own bedroom. Bing was surprised and a little upset, but Nanny was firm and took no notice of the tantrum. I kept my doubts to myself, though I too would have wished otherwise, dreading Tessa's moods and scorn.

After Ready Money, Menabilly seemed very big indeed. Tessa and I explored every room many times and Bing took us out in the gardens and we ran in the woods, enchanted by the space and freedom all about us. Nanny had now to turn cook as well as look after us, and although my mother helped with the fires and chopped wood, she balked at housework – 'Quite unnecessary, all this brushing and dusting, do it once a fortnight,' she told Nanny. She moaned at our untidiness, though. 'How can I make you tidy?' she wailed as we threw our clothes and toys in all directions, Nanny too busy and tired to catch up with us. It was all a little chaotic.

My father was able to get away for a week to visit us at Christmas. The family from Ferryside came and were amazed at how much Bing and Nanny had achieved in so short a time. But Bing, happy to be living at Menabilly, overcame any difficulties in her path, making light of the intense cold and daily grind of keeping us all well and content. As soon as she was able, she settled down to write some short stories, sticking to a strict routine.

She had hired two very young sisters to help in the house, do some cleaning and help Nanny whenever possible. They were called Violet and Joyce and shared a bedroom up a passage beyond Nanny's room. One of them would bring Bing's breakfast up to her bedroom at nine sharp. We would come in for a quick kiss and chat before she took her bath. At ten o'clock she would be seated at her desk in the alcove of her room and be tapping at her typewriter within minutes.

Kits was the only being permitted into her room while she wrote. He would play quietly on the floor with his collection of little lead Red Indians – Laughing Thunder, Grey Wolf and others. At eleven Nanny would creep in and bear him off for his rest, armed with some titbit to keep him quiet. Bing would continue writing until lunch at one o'clock, which she took in a solitary state in the dining alcove; she had firm ideas that children should not eat with grown-ups until they were at least twelve – much better for them to be in the nursery with Nanny.

We would spill into the library when Bing's coffee was brought to her. Kits would scramble on to her lap and pester her and Tessa and I would sprawl on the

sofa telling of our morning. At two o'clock she would
see that we were in need of exercise, so we would all
don coats and boots and go for a good, spanking walk,
exploring new parts of the woods. If the day was fine
and sunny we would demand to go across the lawn to
the beach. If it was wet, we would go down along the
woods, the old drive, the long ride, or the cedar walk,
with its witch's den, an old fallen yew tree across the
path, dark and sinister. Bing would walk with long
strides, dressed in trousers and a jerkin, her hair
blowing about her pretty face, her eyes as blue as the
sea itself. A stick in her hand, she would hit out at the
ever-encroaching nettles and brambles, a constant
battle for our gardener and handyman, Mr Burt.

We would come across Mr Burt, scythe in hand, and
he would pause, mopping his brow with a red spotted
hanky. 'How do, Ma'am,' he would say, 'and how's
my 'andsomes today?' We would stop and chat and
stroke his black mongrel bitch, Yankie. Kits, tired by
now, would want to be going home for tea, so Bing
would gather him up piggy-back fashion and Tessa and
I would run the last bit, breaking out of the wooded
path on to the lawn near the three tall, splendid oak
trees and the gigantic fir. Racing to this tree we would
climb on to the lovely swing Charles Burt had made
us, and back and forth we would go, higher and higher
until cries of 'No, no, Mrs Brown, you'll fall!' would
make us stop and Bing would come into sight with
Kits. We would laugh and push him gently to and
fro. He would gasp with excitement; and suddenly
Bing would sweep him off the seat into her arms,
smothering his face with kisses, saying, 'How's my
boy, my beamish boy,' and we would all troop off to
find Nanny and tea.

I would eat round after round of bread and dripping,

having scorned Nanny's meat loaf at lunchtime. Bing would drink her China tea alone in the library and then go back to write until our bedtime at seven o'clock. She would see to our bath if Nanny was tired or too busy, and after that she would go to her room to change for her dinner. She would put on long house-coats or velvet trousers with a satin blouse and have her drink reading the papers by the library fire.

Kits and I would share a bath to save both time and water. The bath was vast with claw feet, and looked as if it could spring out of the room at any time. The room would steam up and we would slosh around in the bright emerald water for ages, throwing the soap about and making a right old mess. The water came from an old pond, way down in the park by the gates leading to the old drive. It was pumped up some half a mile or so to the house, and although the water did go through a filter of sorts, so that we would not encounter the thick green slime, tadpoles and swan feathers that actually covered the pond, it did stain the sides of the bath and our sponges and flannels, and did very strange things to our hair, much to Nanny's annoyance. The drinking-water came from a pump near the Menabilly cottage in the trees, fifty yards from the front door.

We children were all safely in bed by eight and Tessa was allowed to read till half past. Kits, who was terrified of the dark, had a little night-light on a table between our beds, and was well guarded by his Indians, Laughing Thunder and Grey Wolf. Bing would come in at ten to lift Kits so that he could use his pot. This was to prevent him wetting his bed – we were all too scared to go down the long passage to the loo. Mr Burt had told us of the ghost that haunted Menabilly, a lady dressed in a long blue gown who stared out of the window of the empty room next to my father's dressing-room.

Tessa and I often found it difficult to sleep because of the rats. Menabilly was infested with them, although I never actually saw one. They made their presence felt at night. A battle charge would take place up in the attic. They would dash across our bedroom ceiling, hundreds of pairs of tiny feet scampering, accompanied by the sound of falling masonry and sudden excited squeaks. Although they did not frighten us, they were disturbing. Poor Nanny could not abide the noise, and luckily her room was just out of their range. We did not worry her with the details but instead told Bing, who made up funny stories about the rats which made us laugh, and so we soon became used to them and in time were able to sleep in spite of the din.

We suffered a lot from colds and the bitter weather. The house had no heating and all the rooms were large with high ceilings. The passages and halls were the worst – they were arctic – though we did have well-stacked fires in all the living rooms. I seemed to have chronic earache and would lie in bed with little hot bags of crunchy salt bound to my ears; the pain was awesome.

After the first exciting flush of moving had faded, Nanny's headaches returned and she would take to her bed for days at a time. Bing would try and cope as best she could while the food that Nanny had prepared lasted, but as my mother could scarcely manage to boil an egg or even cut a decent slice of bread without hacking it, Mr Burt's wife would mercifully come to our rescue and cook us tasty stews, using their homegrown chickens and pork. We grew very fond of Mrs Burt, a warm, homely person always as cheerful and smiling as could be.

A few months after our arrival, Bing engaged a retired schoolmistress to give Tessa and me lessons. I remember her with distaste. She was a sour, stern woman and a bully. I hated her. She got on well with Tessa, who egged her on in her dislike of me. The three days she came each week filled me with dread. She wore muddy-coloured clothes and often a rather startling hat perched on her grey locks. Bing would have to hide her smile if they met in the hall, and she made up stories about Laughing Thunder hiding in the bushes ready to spring and attack the silly woman.

Bing often made fun of people behind their backs. She would mock them, making us giggle, say things about them, give them strange make-believe lives – which at times made it very difficult for us children to have respect for our elders. But the times she ridiculed the schoolmistress was grist to my mill.

My dread at lessons was sums. I could not grasp what the wretched woman was saying as she made me stand by her side, her fingers digging into my upper arm. Tessa would clear her throat every time I made one of my many mistakes, and she and the woman would exchange glances, eyes raised to the ceiling. Finally, her patience worn, she would thump me in the back – 'You stupid, stupid child, you silly little dunce' – and I would wish the floor would open up and swallow me up. One day, after a particularly nasty thump on the back, I fled from the room and fainted in the hall. Mrs Burt found me and, as I was dizzy, I went and sat with her in the kitchen until Bing, coming all over 'Mrs Brown', put me to bed for the rest of the day.

Sometimes we had to go to the teacher's home down at St Blazey Gate. It was small and drab and smelt of cats. She shared the house with a younger sister who was small and timid like a mouse, but kind and gentle and in awe of her sibling. The two of us played at shops in a corner, not daring to speak above a whisper and occasionally being afforded sharp suspicious looks from Tessa and Teacher. I felt such relief when the taxi arrived to take us back to Mena. We would leave the car at the top park gates and tear back across the gardens, breathing in the fresh air and freedom.

———————

Bing's novel *Rebecca*, published in 1938, had been a huge success and had in 1940 been made into a film starring Laurence Olivier. *Frenchman's Creek*, published in 1941, had been almost as popular, and had brought many fans in the shape of American GIs to Menabilly. The peace of the gardens became spoilt at weekends by curious Yanks in groups of a dozen at a time, coming right up to the house and saying, 'Say, does the author of *Rebecca* live here?' It was impossible to keep them at bay, and notices of 'PRIVATE KEEP OUT' on the gates had no effect. They came in droves across the park in their jeeps. We even put a sign up saying 'BEWARE THE BUL', but they only pointed out our bad spelling. Like locusts, they would swarm round the house, peering in the windows. Sometimes Bing would hide up on the roof which had a narrow lead parapet all round the edge, just wide enough to crawl along, so she would peep down on the invaders below.

Tessa would be dispatched to deal with them: 'Sorry, Daphne du Maurier is out visiting and won't be back until late.' But there were times when Bing felt she couldn't be rude and unkind in case they were off to fight the next moment and not return. Many would leave books behind to be signed and collected at a later date.

There were one or two naval officers who were very welcome: Richard Aldridge, the husband of the actress

Gertrude Lawrence, and a friend of his, Larry Snell. My Aunt Angela thought the latter wonderful and had quite a crush on him. This made Bing smile and make fun of them, flirting a little herself with the florid-faced, slightly fleshy officer. They used to come to dinner and would always end up seeing us in our night nursery. Richard Aldridge gave us a splendid white woolly toy goat. When you pulled a piece of ribbon in the stomach all sorts of different flavoured chewing gum tumbled out.

The two men sometimes drove us in their jeep down to Pridmouth Beach a mile or so from the house. This was always a great thrill and we would point out little things of interest along the path as we went, proudly showing off the cork trees and then making them use their imagination – 'Down there is the "happy valley" written about in *Rebecca*, full of azaleas in the spring' – and the real-life Grotto full of wonderful shells collected from around the world by the Rashleigh family who owned Menabilly.

The woods and cliffs round Pridmouth Bay were all heavily mined and when going to the beach we were very careful never to wander off the path or beach itself. In a small copse behind the beach a cow had strayed from the nearby field and been blown sky-high – or rather treewards. There it hung by its tail, bloated and stinking, its poor head and horns in another tree, planted there like some cruel hunting trophy; of course we took the two men to view this sight and they held their hankies to their noses, much to our amusement.

At the top of one of the beaches some artificial lakes had been built in the 'happy valley' area. These lakes were lit up every night in the hope that enemy aircraft would mistake them for Fowey. Thank goodness they never did, for Menabilly was very near, to say nothing of the *Rebecca* cottage on the beach beside the bottom lake. A Mrs Garside lived there, custodian of the Grotto.

Nanny was sure that we would all be murdered in our beds by 'that wicked Hitler's bombs'. She ventured into the old part of Mena, and discovered two large vaults on a floor below ground level, lined entirely with lead, with low arched ceilings and stone shelves. These had been the Rashleighs' strong-rooms, used for storing silver and estate papers, for some still had labels stuck on them, items written out in faded copperplate. Nanny got us to help her heave mattresses and blankets and pieces of old carpet down there, and she made two very snug air-raid shelters, lining the shelves with goodies, games and books. As there was no electric light, she stockpiled candles and paraffin heating lamps, torches and boxes of matches, Bing laughed at her efforts, saying she would rather die in her bed than be crushed to death with the whole of Mena on top of her where no one would ever look. In fact, we hardly ever went to them for, with the exception of Bing, we were all far more scared of walking along dusty, empty passages and down the vast, rotten old staircase covered with rat and bat droppings and hearing horrid little scuttling feet than we were of Mr Hitler's air-raids. I remember many years later chancing upon the 'shelters', still equipped with their rusty tins of corned beef and stone bottles of ginger beer.

Fame and the publicity it brought was not welcomed by Bing. She hated it and would shun it as much as she could, but there were times when it was impossible to turn away magazines and the popular press for fear of offending her publishers who wanted the coverage in order to help sell their books. When photographers did come we children were often included in the pictures.

I used to love dressing up in my best frock, the only time now that I ever got to wear a party dress, for we knew no other families, Bing thinking it quite unnecessary to encourage tiresome folk from beyond the park gates. Nanny had long given up the ringlet ritual, but on special occasions she found the time to curl my hair. Tessa, growing taller every day and with plaits halfway down her back, had at last won her battle to wear different dresses, and had Nanny make her something as unlike mine as she could.

Kits would be lovingly dressed by Bing in a sailor-suit, his hair brushed and glowing like Little Lord Fauntleroy, and Bing herself, slim and boyish, would refuse to conform and put on anything other than her beloved trousers. But she would greet the press with a brilliant smile, looking as pretty as a picture, and they would soon be falling over themselves with admiration. We would pose endlessly indoors or in front of Mena, on the lawn, and sometimes down on the beach.

I enjoyed it all until one day, prancing out on to the gravel to welcome a photographer, I was brought to an abrupt halt. 'I suppose you think you're a pretty little girl,' the young man said, camera swinging from his neck. I smiled up at him eagerly, and showed him the tiny pearl necklace given me by my grandmother. He knelt down and looked into my eyes: 'Well, I think you are a spoilt, ugly little horror.' I was amazed by the tone of his voice and unkind expression. I ran into the house and up to our night nursery, seizing my hair-brush and trying to comb out the ringlets, tears streaming down my face. I think I was aged seven at the time. Nothing would induce me to come down. I could hear the man laughing and talking to Bing and Kits below. The photographs were taken without me. The family could not understand my behaviour and I never enlightened them, but the man took away a lot of my confidence for some time. I became more aware of what people said and was quick to react to Tessa's cruel quips.

Bing was longing to get down to serious writing again, and although she had been working on a play, *The Years Between*, and a film treatment for her Irish novel, *Hungry Hill*, her time spent on helping out with certain household chores and Kits had so far prevented any real, new writing. So it was decided that Kits should start doing a morning's lot of lessons with the dreaded Miss R. Tessa and I were put to work at our desks and the teacher produced a large tray filled with sand and got down on her hands and knees beside Kits, who, having been led into the room by Bing, had sunk to the floor and remained rooted to the spot, his toy Indians clutched in a tight little fist. He stared at Miss R with a fierce intensity. A, B and C were carefully traced upon the sand by Miss R and she told Kits to do likewise. He refused to budge, but his colour heightened. The tussle went on for some time until suddenly he stood up and kicked the sand at the woman and shouted loudly: 'That man Hitler will kill you, Mummy says so, so does Laughing Thunder,' and with a hard look at Tessa and me who were stuffing our hankies in our mouths, he stalked from the room. So ended his first and only lesson with the old battle-axe. It was not long after that that the wretched woman had to have her gall-stones out and we were not sorry at all.

CHAPTER SIX

I knew very little about the stresses and strains my parents went through during the war years. We led such a sheltered life out at Menabilly, seeing few people.

In January 1944 my father had been promoted to lieutenant-general and was now in command of the 1st Airborne Corps. In June of that year he supervised the 6th Airborne Division's landing in the Normandy invasion. We seldom saw him, for he could get only occasional leave, arriving and departing like a whirlwind. I do not recall him at all – in fact, trying to remember what he looked like at that time is beyond me. All that remains is a vague image of a uniform, quite faceless, like a paper cut-out. We did get his letters, often written hastily in pencil, difficult to read, sending all his love. He would finish his letters to Bing with 'All the love in a man's heart'; kisses would be sent from his 'Boys', the toy bears he had had from childhood and who had travelled everywhere with him since, packed in a briefcase.

I did not miss him because I did not know him, but I missed the presence of 'a daddy'. I would dwell on the word, the sound it made, and sometimes I would creep into the room he used as a dressing-room, open a drawer and pick up a hanky from the neat pile there, sniffing the faint smell of lavender cologne, lingering. The photograph of the dark-haired man smiling at me from its place on the chest conveyed nothing.

Bing never appeared down or depressed by events going on around her. She had her writing to keep her going and the strict routine of her day in spite of domestic upheavals often sent to try her. She thrived on the isolation of Mena, her quiet evenings alone with a supper tray in the library, the door closed against Nanny and all the children safely tucked up in bed out of the way. She would deal with any correspondence then or read, relaxing away from the typewriter. A new novel had been started based on the Civil War in England, *The King's General*, part fact, part fiction, taking place mostly in Cornwall with Menabilly playing a major role.

When we first came to live at Mena, Bing had discovered a story about a cavalier, a young boy who had been found bricked up in a secret room somewhere near the cellars of the house. Workmen had uncovered the hide-out in the 1920s, and the room had been sealed up, its whereabouts forgotten. The discovery captured Bing's imagination, though, and she began to brew up a plot based on the event.

It was while working on *The King's General* that my mother experienced a strange incident. She was not one to believe much in ghosts or the like, but one summer evening she was getting ready for bed and standing by the open window, the full moon shining in upon the sill, when in the far distance she fancied she heard galloping hooves thundering over the park. They came nearer and nearer and she detected the jingle of a harness and the noise of horses blowing. They came up the hill and she heard metal scraping against metal and hooves stamping beneath her window, hundreds of them, moving round the side of the house. It seemed a whole army was below. She drew back the curtains and leant out. There was nothing there, not a single horse. The moon shone upon the empty gravel drive.

Later, while researching the events of the Civil War in Cornwall, she read that Menabilly was besieged by Cromwellian troops, hunting for Royalists, and that they had camped one night in the park and grounds during a summer night. She never heard the sound again.

Bing liked the feeling of having Mena all to herself in the evenings, to be able to wander from room to room soaking in the atmosphere, sharing the knowledge with past owners and wondering if they loved the house as much as she did. Sometimes, if we couldn't sleep, Kits and I would creep down the stairs and listen to her playing the piano. We would sit on the two little steps leading down to the library, peeping through a chink in the door, spying on her. I would have to restrain Kits from going to her, bribing him with the promise of endless games next day. Bing would always dress for her solitary supper. Gone would be the boyish cords and jerkin; often she wore long, dark embroidered house-coats and, with her shoulder-length fair hair falling over one side of her face, she became a different person to her casual day-time one. Her hair would fall more loosely, and I would be reminded of those beautiful women in *The Tales of King Arthur* waiting for their knights to return from battle, and I would try to imagine the dark-haired man upstairs in the photograph appearing before her, dressed in armour. I would drag sleepy Kits back upstairs, careful not to wake Tessa with her sharp questions. The sound of the tinkling piano would lull me to sleep.

September 1944 was to prove memorable in all our lives. My father had an important role in the Battle of Arnhem, not only in the planning of 'Operation Market Garden' as it was codenamed, but as Deputy Commander of the whole plan to secure bridges over the major water obstacles between Eindhoven and Nijmegen in Holland, in order to facilitate the advance of the armies northwards. It was my father who told Field Marshal Montgomery that they were trying 'for a bridge too far'. He proved to be correct. He never got over the failure of the operation and of the loss of so many of his men.

There was a strange tale he told us about Arnhem. Apparently, each night before the fighting, the German officer of equivalent rank to my father used to send him over a bottle of champagne with a message of 'Good Luck' for the morrow.

The other event that September was that I broke my arm quite badly falling off Polly, Mr Burt's pony. He sometimes brought his son Jim with him to help cut the grass and advancing brambles, and they had the pony to pull the lawnmower. I would pinch apples from the alcove sideboard for Polly, and Jim would allow me to ride her whenever possible, leading me round the paths. The pony suffered from mange and often smelt horribly of the ointment rubbed on her back, so I would then go and roll in the wild garlic, preferring this smell to the other odour. I would trail behind the Burts as they worked about the estate, pestering Mr Burt to tell me stories of the times he had spent up on the Bodmin Moors, breaking in young ponies.

One day I was sitting on Polly's back while she grazed at the far end of the lawn, just out of sight of Mena. Suddenly she bolted, charging back across the grass towards the house, me clinging to her back. I could hear shouts in the background as the Burts saw what was happening. I had never been beyond a gentle trot before and found the galloping quite thrilling, but there was no way of stopping the horse as she only wore a halter. I decided the best thing was to bail off, Indian-fashion, and did so landing head over heels in the long grass. I lay there stunned before an awful pain shot up my arm and I let out a piercing yell. Looking up I saw the red sweating faces of the Burts and Bing as she emerged between them, her face full of apprehension. She had witnessed it all from her bedroom window. I was taken indoors and the doctor came and gave my arm what I thought was a very painful 'Chinese burn' before I passed out. I was given morphine and put to bed.

Bing became very 'Mrs Brown' after my fall and forbade me to go near Polly in future unless she or Nanny was present – 'I can't stand the worry of it all' – as I lay feeling miserable on the library sofa. She brought her typing down and sat tapping beside me all that day, writing some short stories prior to the long, hard slog of *The King's General*. I remember she signed her name all over the plaster of Paris to cheer me up.

It was about this time that she found we were all getting a bit out of hand. Nanny was often in bed with her bad headaches and had to be sent away more frequently to recover, staying with friends near by. Mrs Hancock (Hanks) came to the rescue, doing all the

cooking and trying to cope with all of us. She was
fun and took great trouble, reading us after tea the
Enid Blyton books that Bing refused even to consider
opening. We grew very fond of Hanks and liked to
know that she slept near us, for she used Nanny's
room.

For many years Bing had been corresponding quite
regularly with a Miss Maud Waddell, the woman who
had been governess to the du Maurier children when
they lived in Hampstead. Miss Waddell, nicknamed
'Tod' by Angela, had come down to stay with us several
times at Mena and we liked her very much. Kits took to
her in a big way and told her he was a dog and that she
could call him Snapper. For some time she had had
several posts as governess to different families, but for
the last year or so had been companion to an elderly
couple in Yorkshire, near Thirsk. Bing had been working on Tod to try and get her to come down to
Cornwall, to leave the luxury of Sutton Hall with its
servants and central heating for the rigours of cold
comfort Mena. The matter was decided when the old
gentleman died and Tod was forced to find other
employment.

It was agreed that Tod should come to live at Mena
and take on the task of teaching us three. But first of all
Nanny had to be approached, for the plan might not be
to her liking at all. Bing put it to her very tactfully that
Tod would not be taking her place but would be there
to help her in any way she could. Nanny was delighted
and greeted the news with 'Oh, good, good', for the
thought of another sharing the burden of caring for all
at Menabilly was very welcome indeed.

A flat was made for Tod in the west wing of Mena,
the oldest part of the house, above the old kitchens and
cellars, where the bricked-up cavalier was thought to

have been found. The west wing had been used to store furniture belonging to my father's soldier servant Johnson and his wife, and this was now cleared and a cosy sitting-room, small bedroom and a kitchen with a tiny boxroom were put in order, with good second-hand carpets bought in a local sale by Bing. Nanny ran up some curtains, nice ones, which had belonged to Gran, and a new bathroom was installed on the half-landing of the narrow back stairs below the kitchen. The flat was all complete by the late summer of 1945 and Tod was due on 1 October.

Tessa, Kits and I were all in bed the night we first heard the war was over. Nanny came to tell us and we leapt up with excitement, running down to the library where Bing was sitting reading. We pranced about her yelling, 'The war is over, the war is over!' She put down the paper and rather crossly said, 'I know it is, go back to bed this instant.' We stared, crestfallen and feeling very damped by her strange mood, and crept back to bed. We could not sleep for hours, but we lay chatting and speculating on how soon 'Daddy' would return, the very idea too thrilling to comprehend. Would it be very soon, and was he feeling as delighted as we were, we longed to know.

In the event, my father did not return until the summer of 1946. He had been transferred shortly after Arnhem to the Far East as Chief of Staff to Admiral, Lord Louis Mountbatten, the Supreme Allied Commander. After peace was declared, my father had to stay on in Singapore to plan the demobilization of hundreds of thousands of men, and to deal with the political aspirations of so many of the Asian people. Bing must have been very disappointed at the long delay; she never complained, but she was determined to have *The King's General* published by 1946, for she had dedicated the book to my father as a surprise for him.

A month after the excitement of the war ending, Tod's furniture preceded her by a few days and, on the appointed date, she arrived by train with her heavy luggage; two massive cabin trunks, many hat-boxes, several small suitcases and half a dozen brown paper parcels of varying sizes. Tod was in her mid-fifties, about five feet four and rather plump. She had soft brown hair, cut short and neat, wise china-blue eyes set in a rounded pink and white face, and a no-nonsense mouth and chin. She was not unlike the actress Margaret Rutherford, her voice full and plummy and easy to mimic.

We all gave Tod a terrific welcome and followed her in to show off her new home. She appeared delighted with the layout, praising Nanny's handiwork and Bing's arrangement of the furniture. Tessa and I hovered about in an inquisitive way while she unpacked some of her boxes. We were disappointed by her wardrobe: dull tweed suits of blue and grey, navy wool dresses and many pastel-coloured blouses with Peter Pan collars. She had a few items of jewellery, such as a smooth moonstone brooch and a tiny gold four-leaf clover. On her dressing-table she placed a small pre-war bottle of French Lily of the Valley scent, a box of Elizabeth Arden powder, very pink, and a well-worn lipstick. We did like the smart ivory hair-brushes given to her by Lady Furness, a grateful former employer.

We took more interest in the books and pens and ink brought in readiness for our lessons which were to start a few days later, once Tod had settled in. She brought us wonderful presents of home-made shortbread and rich fruitcake, an unheard-of luxury, sent by her family who lived in New Zealand.

Taking Tod on a tour of the entire house, she soon noted the lack of central heating and I overheard her say to Nanny, 'I cannot abide the cold and I catch chills very easily. I shall have to have a word with Daphne about my bathroom – strikes me it will be like the North Pole in winter.'

She took a week to establish herself and then the day dawned for our first encounter. It was a Monday, and sharp at nine fifteen, watched by Nanny and Kits, Tessa and I walked up the long passage to Tod's front door. 'You may enter' was the reply to our knocking. She was in the kitchen, books lined up on the cleanly scrubbed table, work all set out for our individual requirements. There was a delicious smell lingering in the air of Tod's breakfast of bacon and toast.

I had no fear of saying my tables for Tod, and she even laughed off my stupid mistakes: 'Oh Flavia, dear, we shall soon have this straight,' and Tessa did not mock, at least not for some while. We both enjoyed our work and were willing to try hard. At eleven we had a fifteen-minute break, running around outside in the fresh air, and then we worked until lunch. Tessa had by now been promoted to the dining-room and ate with Bing and Tod. Kits and I remained in the nursery with Nanny, Bing still considering us too young to be of company.

After lunch there were more lessons, and at three thirty Bing took us for a good, brisk walk to 'blow the cobwebs away', and after tea we went up to Tod's flat to do our prep. Tessa sat at the table in the sitting-room while I perched on a small foot-stool near Tod's armchair, and read out loud to her from *The Secret Garden*, a firm favourite, and soon we were in the world of Mary and Dicken.

Kits did not have lessons. Bing said that he would be

going away to prep school at an early age and she wished to spare him as long as she could. He came up to the flat at six thirty to collect us and to see Toddie, as he called her. 'It's Snapper come for the girls,' he shouted as he made his way into the flat, dragging Bing by the hand.

My mother had made it clear to Tod that on no account was she ever to be disturbed in the evening. 'I must have time to myself then,' she said. 'It's what I call the gilt on the gingerbread, these evenings, to sit back and review my day, take stock.' Tod understood completely. She had known her former pupil since she was a child of eleven, and realised long ago Bing's need for space and freedom. During their long correspondence over the years she had grown to respect her feelings. Tod was happy to be up in her flat, cooking her own supper. We would get the delicious smells drifting down the passage, wishing we had had something more exciting to eat than the cup of milk and apple that passed for our dinner.

Nanny, well trained through years of living with Bing, kept to the nursery, working hard at her sewing-machine, half listening to the wireless with an ear out for us up above. And woe betide us if any thumping or bumping was heard on the nursery ceiling, for she would be up in a trice, night-nursery light snapped on to see who the culprit was.

Nanny had been with us now for thirteen years, and there was talk that perhaps it was time she was leaving. We had all grown out of nursery life and she didn't seem to be very happy, what with all her illnesses and constant holidays. We loved her dearly but found her depressed moods more and more difficult to cope with, and she would take offence very easily. As the weeks went by we did tend to spend more time with Tod, for apart from lessons she was such fun and more in with Bing than Nanny had ever been. We did not mean to gang up at all, but we did so dread the days that Nanny was ill.

CHAPTER SEVEN

Sadly Tessa and I did not get on at all well. We either squabbled and shouted at each other or did not speak. I could do no right in her eyes and she nagged at me day and night. Nanny was forever trying to keep the peace. Tod was soon made aware of the atmosphere and was very fair in her treatment of us both. I think she was a little in awe of Tessa who had a sharp tongue and could make very cutting remarks.

We would start our lessons in the morning when suddenly Tessa would bang down her books and declare that my stupid face irritated her so much that she couldn't concentrate. Poor Tod would tut-tut and I would squirm with self-loathing. Tessa would then proceed to build a barricade of books, balancing one upon the other until my face was out of sight. Work would continue till such time as the books or book would be required, and the whole palaver would start again. Tod stood this for some weeks and then finally it wore her down. I was banished with my exercises to the boxroom where Tod kept her trunks.

The room was full of goodies and smelt of wax polish, paraffin and dried flowers. Tod kept her small food larder perched on a table behind the door. It was a wooden box with mesh sides. I would peep inside at the blue china jug full of creamy milk, with its muslin cover held down by tiny red beads at the corners. There was some home-made cream cheese, crisp green cos lettuce, scarlet radishes and round pots of yellow New Zealand butter. Often there was a silver and blue box of Harrogate toffee. I sometimes took a chunk and once Tod came into the room to ask me a question when my mouth was crammed.. I could only grunt and she left, no doubt thinking that I was sulking at having to sit in such dismal surroundings.

The view from the boxroom was unusual. Its lopsided window looked out on part of the nineteenth-century addition where part of the walls had collapsed leaving a fireplace hanging from some gaping masonry, a tree growing from its centre. I would sit gazing at this sight, blissfully alone, away from Tessa's baleful stare.

In the autumn of 1945 Tessa was given two goats by her godmother, which we named Freddie and Doris. They were both nanny goats, but we were determined to call one after my father. They followed us everywhere, even into the house, until one day, returning from a walk, we found them both asleep on Bing's bed, having eaten her silk nightdress and bed-jacket. The goats were very useful in controlling the ever ready brambles that were always threatening to take over. On the good advice of Mr Burt we would take the two of them out on long chains in different parts of the garden. One day while we were having morning break we heard frantic bleats and choking sounds coming from the bushes. Rushing over we found that Freddie had become entangled up round her stake and was on the point of being strangled. Tessa took one look and fled yelling to the house, her arms waving in the air. Quickly and with difficulty, I undid the frantic goat's collar. The rasping stopped and, shaking herself free, Freddie tore after Tessa whom she adored – and I, gazing after her, was butted in the behind by Doris and sent flying.

It was shortly after this episode that a well-known society photographer, Miss Compton Collier, came for the day to capture us all on film. She arrived at eleven, driven by an ancient chauffeur in an even older-looking car, laden down with equipment. Resembling Margaret Rutherford even more than Tod, and dressed in a sweeping tweed Inverness cloak, she alighted at the door with two large cameras on tripods, holdalls full of clanking film plates and a Gladstone bag chock-a-block with squeaky toys to bring smiles to the faces of her victims.

Tessa and I took one look and had to disappear quickly, giggles overcoming us. Bing was not much better and had the utmost difficulty in keeping a straight face. She wore her best linen trousers but Miss Collier, eyeing her up and down, said she had plenty of time to change into a frock. My mother, slightly offended for she thought she looked very smart, declined the offer and stood her ground, whereupon she was told testily that they 'would have to make do and mend'.

The photography session was rather a failure for we could not control our laughter. My mother was all right on her own, but as soon as we were in a group she dissolved. Miss Collier became quite fraught: 'Mrs Browning, do pull yourself together, you are not helping the children one bit by joining in their silly behaviour.' She looked about her wildly for inspiration. 'Have you any pets we could include?' she asked.

'Yes, the goats,' we shrieked, and Tessa and I ran off at top speed to collect them from where they were eating their way through undergrowth near a path called Palm Walk. We undid their chains and they followed us back to the lawn. Miss Compton Collier had gone behind her camera and was completely hidden from the knees upwards by a dense black shroud. Bing was sitting on a rug on the grass brushing Kits' hair. Freddie advanced towards the heaving black shape and rose up on her hind legs, lunged forward, striking from behind. The black form toppled over in a kicking mass and it was difficult to tell legs and tripod apart. Doris, not to be outdone, jumped on the helpless form, bleating in excitement. We all rushed foward and managed to disentangle the poor woman. To give her credit, Miss Collier thought it all quite funny, and the rest of the morning passed more successfully.

After lunch she went into the large dark broom cupboard in the hall to change the plates. This proved too much for us all and the giggles could not be stopped. Bing, with tears of laughter wrecking her make-up, leant against the panelled wall while Tessa and I lay groaning on the floor, holding our aching ribs. Miss Collier emerged from the cupboard ruffled and panting and, seeing us, lost her temper. She dumped the camera on the floor and went in search of her chauffeur.

We hastily pulled ourselves together and tried to make amends. She marched Bing off across the lawn, warning us to keep away from any more sessions, the old chauffeur keeping guard. When she left after tea her mood had improved and she said how much she had enjoyed her day. I remember years later she came to Mena to take some engagement photos of me and it was all I could do not to succumb to the dreaded giggles once more.

Looking back on our war years at Mena I realise what a lonely life we must have led. We were sometimes allowed to mix with other children but Bing loathed the thought of having to meet other young parents, believing it would upset her writing routine. Although she had learned to drive as a girl she had never kept it up, so the only means of transport was by taxi. We did on occasion play with the local village children, but this was frowned on by Bing and Tod. They were never encouraged to come anywhere near the house, so we had to sneak out and meet them in the woods.

Tessa suffered most of all. There was no real outlet for her bright, intelligent mind. Tod did her best during lesson-time and my father's sister, Aunt Grace, who came to stay quite often, made a fuss of her, trying to bring her out of herself, but that was about the limit. Because Tessa and I got on so badly, I was thrown into doing everything with Kits, four years my junior, and this resulted in me remaining incredibly childish for my age. Bing and Nanny encouraged our togetherness for it saved them having to deal with Kits so much. He was hopeless on his own for long, always demanding company, a constant playmate, so there I was; and it now was a complete habit to lump us together.

Bing despised girlish ways and, as I was no longer under Nanny's influence, I strived to please my mother in the way I dressed. I was dressed in cord trousers and boys' shirts, my hair cut straight and bobbed. Dolls were mocked, bikes and toy cars promoted, and football and cricket pushed to the fore as Kits grew older. I developed into a tomboy, climbing trees and exploring deep into the Mena woods.

Tessa, twelve years old, became more isolated. She would go for long walks on her own with Freddie and Doris trotting after her, and no one seemed to care. She told me years later that she used to sit in the loo wondering how she could commit suicide. Nobody had any idea she was so unhappy. She says three things stand out in her mind about her childhood at Mena: the cold, the hunger and the wretched rats; and I suppose you could add loneliness.

Once more we did indeed fare quite badly where food was concerned. Nanny, who was a good cook, rapidly gave in because of ill-health and exhaustion. On the bleak days she remained in her darkened room and we had the usual bread and dripping until Hanks came to the rescue. But Tod took a dim view of Hanks' cooking. Looking at the small, sparse lamb cutlets on the sideboard, Tod would mutter, 'What short commons, very different from the good fare at Sutton Hall.' Bing, seeing nothing amiss, would glance at Tod surprised, and smile sweetly. She seldom found fault with the food for she was not interested. Tod would protest that she could 'live off the smell of an oil rag'.

The only outings we ever had, apart from going to see my grandmother, were birthday treats, when Bing would take us all to the Red Lion in Truro. The taxi ride usually made Kits and I feel sick and when we got there we were too excited to eat much, though Tessa made up for lost time, cramming as much as she could into her mouth.

Once we were taken up to London by train to see the play *Peter Pan*, the actress Mary Morris playing Peter. The book was a great favourite of ours for it had been written for my Great-Aunt Sylvia Llewellyn Davies's children. My grandfather, Gerald du Maurier, had played the first Captain Hook. We loved our visit and the good food in London.

When we returned I nearly hanged myself trying to fly like Peter Pan. I leapt from a high branch in a tree with a rope fastened about my waist. Unfortunately, the rope had slipped up to my neck and I was rescued just in time by Mr Burt. I made him swear never to tell Bing, because 'Mrs Brown' would have had a fit. The kindly man never did let on, I'm thankful to say.

My mother's play, *The Years Between*, which she had written in 1944, was successfully produced in the West End and although we had begged to see it she naturally declared it unsuitable for children. The film of *Frenchman's Creek*, which came to Troy Cinema, Fowey, was likewise thought not fit for our young eyes. There was quite a do at the little cinema to celebrate the opening of the film. They had a gala night which Bing attended, all got up in a long dress, and most of the county went, bent on catching a glimpse of the shy author. We thought that she looked like a film star herself as she was driven off in a taxi, and she had been duly fêted by the remaining American soldiers.

I celebrated my ninth birthday in April 1946. For weeks leading up to the day I had been pestering Bing for a pony of my own. Whenever I was able to catch her alone I would plead, 'Please, please,' and every night I prayed, kneeling by my bed, Kits looking on with great interest. Bing did not seem very interested, saying it would be too difficult to look after a pony, that I would forget to feed her and so on. I decided it was no good, so I asked for a Crucifix and a large penknife instead, a request Bing found very funny, roaring with laughter to Aunt Angela about it on the telephone.

On the morning of my birthday I did get those two items, and Kits and I were playing with the knife out on the lawn when we heard footsteps coming along the path through the trees behind Menabilly cottage. Glancing up, I saw Mr Burt coming out of the shadows leading a small brown pony. They came down the incline towards us and Kits gave a wild whoop and grabbed me by the hand. I was rooted to the spot. 'Look, Beaver,' he shouted my nickname, 'Look, Beaver, it must be for you, your birthday present!' Mr Burt led the pony up to us and I saw that it had a white star on the forehead. I heard the creak of the new leather saddle and the clink of the bridle as the pony softly champed the bit. I heard a scraping on the gravel and there stood Bing, a large smile on her face, and behind her Tod and Nanny beamed across at me.

Polly – I could think of no other name – was a Bodmin Moor pony, aged ten and with a will of her own. She sized me up very quickly and got her priorities right: it was to be a master and slave relationship and I was soon a willing slave. Mr Burt taught me how to mount and dismount and how to lead Polly, and then I was on my own. A stable had been made for her round the back of the house in part of the old coach-house, and a paddock fenced off at the far end of the front lawn.

I soon discarded the saddle and rode bare-back, sometimes with a blanket, Indian-fashion. I worshipped Polly and was with her whenever possible. Poor Kits suffered and would trail after us, pleading with me to play with him. I would sometimes spare an hour or so and his face would light up and he would let me choose the game, a sop to curry favour.

Bing became very fond of Polly, nicknaming her 'Girla' for some reason. She would let me ride in the park as long as she was with me, and would stand with Kits at her side giving me half-hearted instructions, difficult to follow without the aid of a saddle. I would charge them at the gallop, nearly knocking them for six till she yelled, 'Stop, stop, Mrs Brown!'

CHAPTER EIGHT

Nanny eventually left us in the late summer of 1946. She went away to stay with friends and did not come back. It was a sad ending and we missed her, although of late she had remained very much in the background because of illness. Bing gave her a substantial sum of money in the hope that she would start up a small business making children's clothes, as she sewed so well. This she never did, but after a long break she took up further positions as nanny to other families and was very happy. She did occasionally come back and take Kits and me on short holidays to St Ives and to stay with Granny at Rousham. She is alive today, well into her eighties, though I have not seen her for many years.

My father was forty-nine when he returned from the Far East in September 1946. His new job was that of Military Secretary to the Secretary of State for War, which required him to live in London. Bing refused to move, so he planned to come to Mena every weekend, taking the night train on Friday evenings. His sister,

Aunt Grace, had rented a small flat off the King's Road in Chelsea, and invited him to share this with her during the weekdays, which he did.

Tessa and I do not recall his first visit back to Mena, though Kits can remember being shouted at for touching some yachting papers and running from the room in tears. I do know that at first he did not take very much interest in us, seeming bored by the children he had left behind. Nor did he show much enthusiasm for Mena and his surroundings, much to Bing's great anguish and disappointment.

My father was just under six foot, slim, with slightly receding dark hair, fine green eyes, and a handsome, strong face with a neat military moustache. He was always immaculately dressed – even when wearing casual boating clothes he was spick and span. He was not one to suffer fools and we children soon became in awe of him, and often quite frightened. He had a quick temper, sometimes almost screaming with rage, but then it would all fizzle out and he would be smiling and bright, his anger forgotten.

He was not keen on young children, easily irritated by them, and often said they should be seen and not heard. But he became very proud of Tessa's looks as she was so pretty and had an engaging manner with grown-ups, seeming much older than her years. He called me 'Old Gumpet' and more than once I heard him say how plain I was – 'Plain as a pikestaff,' he would laugh and he was right: my lank hair and gappy teeth were not appealing. He took almost no interest in Kits, being jealous of his son's closeness to Bing and of her great love for him.

But there were times when we had fun with him, when his mood was good. This was at bath-time at the weekends, usually a Saturday night. He would fill the large bath with the green water and Kits and I would sit at either end. The bath was often full of toy boats, as at one time we had a fleet of lead battleships – most painful if sat on – and my father would bomb us with a very big, wet sponge which he held high above his head to get the maximum effect. He taught us a mad bathing song which we all sang at the top of our voices, and soon the steam made it impossible to see across the room. Water got everywhere and very little washing got done till suddenly my father would descend on us, sponge full of suds, and begin scrubbing us for all he was worth. He must have become soaked in the process. It all came to an end when Bing shouted above the din that supper was ready. It was then that we got our own back for, dashing down to the drawing-room in dressing-gowns, we would have a pillow fight with him.

My father would have changed by then into an elegant wine-coloured velvet smoking-jacket and trousers. He would stand in the middle of the floor, hands on his bent knees, and fix us with a challenging glare. We would seize cushions off the sofa and whack him hard about his immaculate head. His smoothly brushed hair would stand out like a ruffled owl's feathers, the sight of which would send us into fits of laughter, collapsing on the floor with weakness. We would then race upstairs and hide in the night nursery, on the window seats behind the curtains. He would follow slowly, humming as he went like some strange bee. Our nervous giggling let us down and he would grab one of us and throw us over his shoulder, shouting out 'Any old coal, any old coal!'.

Kits and I had now been promoted to the dining-room following Nanny's departure. This was a mixed blessing for our table manners were not of the best, and again things depended on my father's mood. If he was in a jolly frame of mind, well and good: he would hold forth on politics, local events and his boats. No one else got much of a word in except Tod, the only one brave enough to voice an opinion. Kits and I would stay mute, in case picked on. Bing, if she was brewing on a story, would sit at her end of the table, picking at her food and staring into space, a vacant look on her face. My father would suddenly pounce and ask her a question: 'Well, what do you think, Duck?' (They called each other Duck.) She would drag herself back to the present: 'Well, I can hardly say, Duck,' she would reply, a faint smile on her face. My father would look down the table at her and thunder, 'Woman, you live in a dream!' which indeed she did when working hard on some novel or other. My father would cast an eye round the table, ready to claim his next victim.

Tod and he did not see eye to eye, though they had a healthy respect for each other; but were both jealous of Bing, vying for her attention. One Sunday lunch Tod was suffering from a bad cold. We were seated at the table, watching my father carve the leg of lamb. Tod turned to Bing. 'Daphne, dear, I have such a sore throat, what shall I do?' she asked.

My father turned round from the sideboard and, carving-knife in hand, he looked at Tod, his green eyes glinting: 'My dear Tod, why don't you cut it?' he said, offering her the carving knife.

Poor Tod, very flushed in the face, rose from the table: 'Tommy, that remark ill becomes you and was neither clever nor funny,' and she stalked from the room. We could hear her ascending the stairs and the loud bang of her flat door.

'Silly old arse, bellyaching like that,' my father said

My mother, Daphne du Maurier

We hardly knew my father when we were children

We knew my father's mother,
Anne Browning, as Granny

We loved visiting Granny at
Rousham

Gran, my mother's mother,
at Ferryside

Gran with one of her beloved
pekinese

Aunt Angela,
my mother's elder sister

Aunt Jeanne,
my mother's younger sister

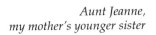

*Aunt Grace holds
me at Rousham*

*Nanny took the place of
my mother when she
returned to Egypt*

Tessa holds her newborn sister

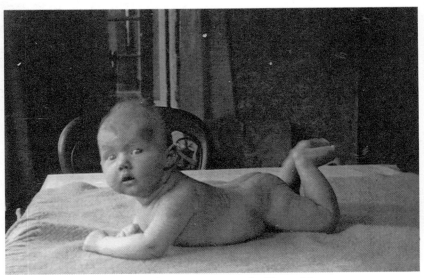

Kits was the son my parents had longed for

My mother with her two daughters at Greyfriars

It would be many years before Tessa and I became friends

Tod, our governess

*Tessa rarely played with
Kits and me*

*Kits sailing a boat in
Dr Rashleigh's Bath*

*At Pridmouth Bay: me,
Tessa, my mother, Kits*

My father's yacht, Jeanne d'Arc

Kits and I dreaded
sailing on the Fanny Rosa

*Above left: Kits was
my mother's favourite*

*Above: My parents said
I was 'as plain as a pikestaff'*

*Left: Tessa was
grown-up for her age*

as he helped himself liberally to mint sauce. Tod remained in her flat until he departed for London that night and the following weekend he was made to apologise by Bing. 'I must eat humble pie, I suppose,' he grumbled, taking a stiff swig of gin and lime prior to the encounter. My father got on with people very well, and with his great charm and good manners most women found him irresistible. Tod was the only one not won over by his magnetism.

Bing was always very easy-going with everyone. She hated to hurt or offend people and was wonderful at putting folk at their ease. When my father brought down to Mena the young woman who had been his personal secretary out in the Far East, Bing welcomed Maureen into the family.

Maureen Luschwitz was about twenty-one and very pretty, with a cloud of dark hair. We all took to her immediately and as she had no family in England she was encouraged by Bing to spend her holidays with us at Mena. Kits and I thought she was the greatest fun, and she joined in all the goings-on at Mena with enthusiasm. Later on, she would prove to be of enormous help to us during our school years, taking care of us when in London and often meeting school trains. Tod was more difficult to please; she liked to rule the roost and was a trifle too bossy to Maureen on occasions. There were days when Tod's 'hard chairs' would take over, but they never lasted long. Bing would always see to that – she hated anyone to feel unhappy and left out.

In the summer months my father would spend most weekends on his beloved boat *Ygdrasil*, a small cabin cruiser whose name in Norse mythology means 'Tree of Fate'. It was in *Yggy* that my father first saw Bing: as he was motoring up Fowey harbour he had noticed a lovely blonde girl sailing in a small yacht in the opposite direction. And it was in *Yggy* that they spent their honeymoon, up the Helford river at Frenchman's Creek.

Often we would all go aboard, leaving Tod alone at Mena as she disliked the sea. Old Hanks would make us crisp pasties – bacon ones for Kits and me, as we hated the usual meat – wrapped up in stiff white damask napkins, and we would drive in to Fowey in Old Fordie, my father's runabout, and be met at the slipway or yacht club by Mr Bunt, a retired seaman who looked after the boat. He would row us out in the pram to where *Yggy* was at anchor in the harbour.

We enjoyed going up the River Fowey to Pont or Lerryn if the tide was right. Going ashore to stretch our legs after our picnic lunch, my father would search the trees and water for rare glimpses of unusual birds – both he and Bing were keen ornithologists – and we would be delighted if he spied something special. 'Quick, look, Duck, over there,' one would say, and they would raise their field glasses and chat excitedly, my father drawing hard upon his cigarette. *Yggy* was very cramped inside her small cabin, so fine days were a bonus. Mr Bunt and my father would endlessly discuss boats and the yachts they hoped to build one day, Bing sometimes sitting a little hunched in the stern. The faraway expression on her face would occasionally catch my father's eye, and he would smile his crooked grin and say in a light, bantering tone, 'Mummy will pay for him to have a goodly boat, won't she, all those film rights put to good use?' She would shrug her shoulders and feign indifference, but already planning how she could give him the boat of his dreams. In the years which followed the film rights came in very handy indeed.

We would spend all day on the water and in the early

evening call in on Gran at Ferryside for a drink before returning home.

Kits and I dreaded having to go outside the harbour if the sea was at all choppy, for then we would be as sick as cats. We began yawning and going green within minutes, much to my father's disgust. Poor Bing anxiously kept an eye on us, dreading lost tempers and harsh words. She never became cross herself but understood our feelings, sometimes a little queasy herself, lying taking deep yoga breaths, willing my father to turn about and annoying him by her lack of interest in her surroundings.

Tessa was a good sailor and seldom ill. She and my father would complain about us, saying, 'Those loons are hopeless,' using their nicknames for us. He bought her a sailing-boat, a small yacht called *Shimmer*, a deep-keeled eighteen-foot craft of the local Troy class. There were twelve of these – *Shimmer* was number four – and they raced against each other every Wednesday afternoon and Saturday.

My father had also bought a large CFV. This he had seen in Singapore and had had brought back on a troop ship and refitted out in Hunkin's yard in Fowey over at Bodinnick. *Fanny Rosa* was painted a striking blue-green, and had rust-coloured sails. She could sleep six, being very broad in the beam. But she had one great disadvantage: she rolled; even in the calmest waters at anchor she rolled. It was possible to get used to this quirk though it was not very restful, and for Kits and me it was disastrous. When there was a bit of a swell our fate was sealed.

We went in *Fanny Rosa* along the coast to Pool; Kits and I lay prone on our bunks the entire trip, both of us wishing we were dead, my father spitting with rage as he had arranged the trip as a lovely treat for us all. Pool harbour is not one of the most sheltered havens, the sea often fairly choppy across West Bay. The next day, to add insult to injury, we made Bing take us back by train – so shaming – but I'm glad to say that Tessa joined us, though somewhat sheepish.

My father invented a game for us that he called 'Monkey Skin'. It was a mini-Olympic Games. We were quite brilliant at running about on all fours like a monkey, and when my father saw us doing this he gave a shout of laughter and stamped his foot, tears streaming down his face.

'Monkey Skin' took place in the Long Room, once a games room and now the most beautiful drawing-room, forty feet long, with a deep orange carpet. After the grown-ups had had their supper, Moper would come up to the nursery and say it was the night for 'Monkey Skin'. We would leap out of bed, trembling with excitement. There would be four events, all organised and planned by my father.

First of all was boxing. He had bought us tiny boxing-gloves and Kits and I each wore a pair of his silk hurdling shorts, tied at the waist with Old Etonian and Eton Rambler ties. We were bare-chested and wore no shoes. Bing, slightly put out by the fact that we should be tucked up in bed, nevertheless moved her chair forward to get a ringside view, and Tessa did likewise, though carefully held a paper up in front of her face, sighing loudly. The boxing match had two bouts of four rounds, and we took it in turns to win, this arranged hurriedly beforehand.

Then it was the hurdle race of cushions down the length of the room. My father had taught us to hurdle and was keen that our style was correct. As I was faster than Kits, I had to either slow down or fall over, depending on my mood. This was followed by the long-jump which took place over a white linen tablecloth spread across the carpet, my father standing by with tape measure at the ready . . . By this time Tessa was making rude remarks, but was quickly quelled by us all. The highlight of the evening was the show-jumping, an arduous course over many cushions arranged by my father while we practised out in the hall. We would be called in one at a time and would gallop for all we were worth on all fours, easily clearing obstacles of three foot or so.

The winner was presented with a silver cup which my father had won in his youth when at Eton. In the audience, seated on small blue cane chairs were 'The Boys', my father's teddy bears, safely back from the war and sporting new ribbons bought by their proud owner. The second prize was two shillings, usually asked to be returned next day to go towards the cigarette fund – 'A chap is clean out of cash' – so you could kiss goodbye to that small prize.

If we played our cards right and did nothing to irritate, my father allowed us to stay for a while. He would put on the radiogram and play some of the ballet music of which he was so fond – *Swan Lake* or *Sleeping Beauty* – or sometimes the latest long-player of an American musical which we always had sent over from Bing's publishers in New York. I would sit beside my father on the sofa and he would hold my hand, and sometimes stroke my hair, calling me his Old Gumpet. I was careful not to catch Bing's or Kits' eye, for they, squashed together in an armchair, were quick to mock, pulling faces to make me laugh, nudging each other. It was rare to have a moment of closeness with my father for neither parent was very tactile. I would have been much too embarrassed to make a move in their direction.

The war was over but nothing seemed to change very much at Mena, though we did have the occasional drama. The land-mines along the coast and down at Pridmouth were being cleared. We would watch the men going off through the Mena woods with all their equipment, and one day while Kits and I were playing out on the lawn we heard a terrific bang. Some time later a group of men appeared from the direction of a path to the left of the house carrying a reclining figure. We rushed forward and saw a man covered in blood, his leg half torn away. I can remember his chalk-white face and blank, staring eyes. We ran indoors to alert the grown-ups and the little group were taken to the library and the man placed on the sofa to await the ambulance. His blood had dripped on to the white carpet and left a rust-coloured stain.

As soon as the area surrounding the beach was made safe we would often go down to Pridmouth for picnics and swimming. We would spend long, lazy days there, often making for the stretch of rocky coast just below the path that wound up towards the Gribbin. To get to our favourite corner we had to pass a narrow inlet and small sandy beach, and in the shallows of the water lay the wreck of an old cargo ship. She had come aground in thick fog in the early 1930s, a scene witnessed by Bing, and which gave her the idea in *Rebecca* of the ship foundering and so leading to the discovery of Rebecca's yacht. We would climb over the broken old hulk, often scraping our skin on the sharp pieces of rusting metal, but it was good fun and we had many a pirate fight on her.

On fine sunny days, Gran and Angela, now nick-named 'Piffy', would come out for lunch at Mena and in the afternoon we would go down to the beach to swim. At twelve thirty on those days Kits and I would go to the park gates to await Gran's arrival, swinging on the open gates and listening out for the sound of the Hillman roaring across the park in second gear – for Gran had never learnt to drive, and the gears remained a complete mystery to her. She would slow down as she approached the park gates, blow shaky kisses to us and then charge up the short drive having at last found fourth gear. The car would come to a shuddering stop at the front door.

Gran was not one for walking very far, and if she could she would demand to take the car down the path to Pridmouth beach. It was a hilly, single-track road, lined with old tank tracks. My father, if he was about, would say, 'God help you all,' a little too loudly, and the thought of Gran taking the car to the beach always filled us with dismay.

Bing would be made to 'volunteer' to go in the car with her, taking the picnic tea and Tod with her painting things. Tod liked to sketch and do watercolours of the coast and sea. Kits and I would run ahead, with Tessa and Piffy bringing up the rear, walking sedately and gossiping.

We would arrive long before the others and spend a while seeking out and bagging a good sheltered picnic spot. The others' journey down was usually uneventful, the car often in neutral, Gran pumping the brakes at jerky intervals.

Once she was installed on the beach we would be told to disappear to the other bay round the rocks while Gran had her dip in the sea. She couldn't swim but would advance into the water up to her shoulders and, with her feet encased in white rubber strap shoes, would step along on tip-toe, making breast-stroke movements with her arms. When we first witnessed this, we let out such yelps of hysterical laughter that poor Gran was put off her so-called swim for weeks, so we had been banned from the scene. We would wander back as she was discreetly changing behind a suitable rock, the large wet bathing-dress lying large as a black cat at her feet. Once dressed and refreshed, she would come and watch us sail our toy boats in the lovely rockpools nearby, particularly in a deep, oblong one which we named Dr Rashleigh's Bath, my mother pretending that the old chap sat in it when in residence.

We would sit munching our tea which usually consisted of rounds of egg and tomato sandwiches. I remember on one outing Tod sat on the tomato sandwiches, squashing them to a pulp. Gran, who was partial to these, was very short with her, her quick temper flaring up. Poor Tod, very pink in the face, was most humble and kept muttering 'Beg pardon', like Uriah Heep.

On the return journey up the path, Gran would take half an hour turning the car to face the right direction. This manoeuvre would attract some unwanted attention. At the sound of the wild revving of the engine, other bathers and picnickers would run up from the beach, and in no time there would be a sizeable crowd. Gran, flustered and getting more and more cross, would make a tremendous effort. Foot well pressed down on the accelerator, she would bravely put the Hillman into fourth gear, forgetting to also put her foot on the clutch. The gear would shriek and grind in protest and shouts of advice would filter through to Gran, and she would groan and lose her already frayed temper. She did not take criticism from what she called 'the lower orders'. Wrenching at the gear she would at last manage to move the car forward in bumpy, jumpy bounds. Once she had got going she would leave nothing to chance and would continue in like fashion until she reached the front door of Mena, where my father would stalk over to her, saying, 'What's this frightful bloody stink of burning rubber?'

When Gran and Aunt Angela left us to go home, Kits and I were often made to go up to the top park gates to save Piffy getting out of the car to open them. Scorning a ride in the Hillman, we would tear along on our bikes, getting the gates open just in time as Gran rushed past at breakneck speed on to the open road.

We had made friends with the grandchildren of an old lady called Mrs Viall who lived in the Menabilly cottage. About a hundred yards away looking out towards the park, the small house was perched on a slight rise and behind it was the ruin of the old Menabilly stables. The two grandchildren, Geraldine and Nadia, were about our ages, and if they saw us in the park they would run down to the second gate to talk to us. The younger girl, 'Noddy' as we nicknamed her, became Kits' devoted playmate. Instead of always getting me to play with him, he now had a willing friend at his beck and call. In the mornings after breakfast he would rush out on the gravel in front of Mena and bark loudly like a dog. Noddy would respond from over at the cottage with a high-pitched yelp, and within seconds she was running over, ready to play any game which her hero had chosen. On long, hot summer days she would toil on the lawn, bowling non-stop to Kits but seldom being allowed to bat, and on cold winter days there she would be, kicking endless balls towards Kits' goalposts. Bing and I thanked our lucky stars for little Noddy. She saved me from having to play with him and it stopped Bing from fretting whether Kits had too lonely a time.

When we became friends with a small gang of children from the little hamlet and local farms, Bing was not so amused. She would tell us off quite sharply and threaten us with early bed, the worst fate, if we played with these children. She called them 'honks', and I suppose was as bad as Gran over what she referred to as a 'different class'. Tod was her ally in this and we had to be careful when giving them the slip.

The house and grounds were so large that it was easy to disappear for a while without fear of being caught. Kits and I would creep out of the old kitchen and go round the back of the house to the woods beyond. A vast old spreading chestnut tree we called Sherwood was our meeting-place. The gang of about five or six would arrive led by their leader, a small red-haired, freckle-faced boy called Peter. Armed with sticks and knives we would explore deep into the Mena woods, often forgetting all about the time. We made splendid houses in the dense bamboo thickets which grew in profusion along the old drive, hideouts known only to ourselves. We swung like Tarzan from thick ivy ropes hanging in the trees, and discovered giant rhubarb-like plants with leaves six-foot wide in the swampy area above the artificial lakes, and we rolled and fought mock battles in the sea of wild white garlic that covered much of the ground in spring and summer.

Whooping and yelling we chased each other further into the woods to the darkest recesses, frightening the pigeons and sometimes ourselves, sharing out any sweets or goodies we might have about our persons. Then, if someone was lucky enough to own a watch, we would suddenly realise what time it was and back we would go, the fight knocked out of us, a mad thirst taking hold. We would drift back to Sherwood and call goodbye to the gang and wander back along the side lawn, smoothing our ruffled appearance, ready with a casual shrug and quick fib if questioned. Cold water drunk from a cup, much more refreshing than from a glass, would see us right, and we would go and lie on the nursery floor well pleased with our outing.

In the heart of the Menabilly woods was an old cottage called Southcott, once a dwelling for game-keepers. It stood in a small clearing, a little way off the old drive. During our play we always gave this place a wide berth. Isolated as it was, two elderly ladies lived there, a Miss Phillips and her companion, Miss Wilcox. The former had been private secretary to old Dr Rash-leigh, the owner of Mena. Kits and I thought the couple most sinister, this belief elaborated by Bing with her usual make-believe stories of their life. Rumour had it that they were spiritualists.

If we were biking in the park we would sometimes see the two women return from shopping, walking arm in arm towards the entrance in the park to the old drive. It was a fair way to have to go, and once we biked up to them and asked if they would like some help with their bags. Their black mongrel dog stood guard, low growls coming from its open jaws. Miss Phillips, her hair very white in the sunlight, turned her mystical-looking blue eyes on us and bowed slightly, a faint smile twitching her lips as if she thought our offer amusing. It was Miss Wilcox, tall and stout, with her thick grey hair wound in plaits round her ears, who spoke: 'Be off with you young scamps, you haven't the strength,' and she peered at us through the thick pebble glasses and laughed loudly, a deep, harsh sound which made their dog bark.

Tod became friendly with them both and would tramp down to Southcott for tea, taking a basket of goodies like Red Riding Hood visiting her grand-mother. They were about the only folk poor Tod ever saw to give her a bit of conversation and company. When Miss Phillips returned her call she had to go up the narrow back stairs to the flat in case she should bump into Bing, who never thought of inviting her to tea.

Tod was very busy during school hours now, for it had been decided by my father and his sister Grace that it was time Tessa went away to boarding-school to be with girls her own age and to get a wider education than Tod was able to offer. St Mary's, Wantage, was chosen as Aunt Grace knew the Mother Superior and the school was near to Rousham and Granny Browning. Tessa was overjoyed at this news, and she and Tod started to get ready for the common entrance exam.

I spent all the lesson time in Tod's boxroom, doing set work which Tod had planned for me. Half the time I just sat and stared out of the window and covered pages of my exercise book with drawings of horses. Now and then I would slip out down the back stairs and go out to Polly, jump on her back and have a quick canter along the Palm Walk, often ending up in her paddock, and sneaking up to where Bing had her writing hut overlooking the sea and Gribbin headland. This hut, painted green and hidden at the back by tall bushes, had an iron bench under the large window. I would sit on this and listen to the brisk tap tapping and occasional throat-clearing and wonder during the short pauses when all was still whether Bing was far off in her 'never never land' surrounded by the characters who peopled her books. Polly would wander over to me and my mother, seeing the pony, would call out, 'Hello Girla old thing,' and I would run quickly, too fearful of detection, for once or twice I had been observed when Bing had come out to light a cigarette and stretch her limbs and she had, without fuss or scolding, told me to return to Tod. Her smile and gentle voice made me feel very guilty and when I apologised, she had dismissed me with a light laugh, saying, 'I do so see your point, lovey, but old Tod will worry, so run off now before she finds you out.'

So back I would go to clamber up the steep little back stairway and take my seat in the boxroom. Tod was never the wiser and Bing never divulged my sorties.

CHAPTER NINE

On wet days we would explore the north wing of Mena, the empty part, added in the late 1890s. These adventures were frowned on by Bing as it was considered unsafe with all the dry-rot flourishing in most quarters. At the end of our drawing-room was a strong white panelled door leading to this old part. We would steal the key and go through, locking the door behind us.

The building was on three floors, and the first room we came to on the right-hand side on the ground level was the old library. This was a fine large room with a high ceiling and three big sash windows facing the side lawns. The room was dry and the walls were lined with beautiful oak bookcases, many filled with an assortment of family books. The room was used for storing Browning and du Maurier stuff. There were two vast cabin trunks, their items spilling out of the half-open drawers: long, yellowing gloves to fit a tiny hand; dull, sticky costume jewellery with bits missing; faded lavender bags, their contents grey and brittle;

neat piles of ivory-coloured tissue paper; pink moth-
balls; a wisp of pale blue chiffon scarf and torn oyster
satin handkerchief covers. There was a painting of Bing
on the walls, a very bad likeness which we had used at
some time for target practice with our bows and arrows,
the face all pitted with holes as if she had a bad case of
measles.

We would play hide and seek, carefully checking on
entering the other rooms to make sure the floors were
safe. All the rooms had fine carved mahogany doors,
heavy wooden shutters and lovely marble chimney-
pieces. The walls had delicate Victorian flowered wallpaper with wide, pretty borders. Rotting brocade bell-
pulls hung from the walls, ending in tarnished brass
tassels. There were thick black cobwebs in the corners,
and the dusty floor was covered in bat droppings and
the dried wings of dead butterflies. The lavatories had
wide panelled mahogany seats with dark blue willow-
patterned bowls and flowered hand-basins. In some
rooms the ceilings had collapsed in on the floor and
horrid orange fungi sprouted amongst the rubble. On
the lower ground floor, near to our air-raid shelters,
striking green ferns grew out of the walls and thrust
their way through broken windows. The whole place
smelt both damp and dusty. We felt sorry for the house
so little lived in, dying of decay and neglect. Once we
had finished our game we did not wish to linger, for a
sense of gloom and sadness overcame even our childish
spirits, and suddenly the silence and shadows made us
want to scurry back to our older, but more lived-in
house.

In later years the top floor of the north part was
known by us all as the King's Road. About four of the
larger rooms became chock-a-block with du Maurier
and Browning furniture, pictures, glass, china and bric-

à-brac. It was an Aladdin's cave. Bing, who had no interest in material possessions, gave carte blanche to the family and close friends to come and take their pick. And indeed they did – some, with hindsight, more than others. But there would be moments as time went by that elderly aunts, when on a visit to a nephew or niece, would suddenly be confronted by a piece of favourite furniture and ask, 'Where did you get that desk/picture? It's strictly mine,' and much confusion and embarrassment would result. The Rashleigh family, who returned to Mena in the late 1960s, finally demolished the north part and nothing now remains of those stately, decaying rooms, Nanny's air-raid shelter and the King's Road.

The harsh winter of 1946 nearly did for us all at Mena. The cold was truly awful. We might as well have been in Siberia. All the pipes froze throughout the house for weeks. Water had to be carried from the fresh-water pump over by Mrs Viall's cottage. Kits and I used to go to bed with all our clothes on, and even with two stone hot-water bottles and heaps of blankets, we shivered and shook. The electricity went off for days at a time, and we were very glad of Nanny's stockpile of candles, enough to withstand a siege, in the air-raid shelter. We had Aladdin oil-lamps in every corner of every room and passage, kept well filled by Mr Burt, but an awful fire risk. We did not wash for days and lived on stews cooked on a tiny calor gas fire.

The house was completely snowed in. Tod's flat felt like the North Pole and she had to move down to sleep in my father's dressing-room, and we did our lessons in the room adjoining, known as the Blue Lady room, because it was here that the ghost was said to have been seen. It was a large pleasant room above the drawing-room and snug and warm because the two fires in the latter were kept well banked up night and day.

We did get some fun out of the hard conditions, playing in the snow and building giant snowmen, and we tobogganed on tin trays in the park, and even tried skating on the frozen lakes at Pridmouth until Bing was overcome by 'Mrs Brown'. The goats spent much of their time indoors with us, smuggled in upstairs to Tessa's bedroom, for she now slept on her own in a room above the kitchen beyond the room Violet and Joyce shared. Tessa had an awful job keeping Freddie and Doris quiet. They would bleat loudly with joy and then frustration. We tried gagging them with socks and scarves but these they ate in no time.

One day Tessa left her door open by mistake and the goats somehow found their way to my father's dressing-room. He went into this and found them happily eating their way through a favourite old coat that had belonged to his father. We were all down in the hall when we heard a bellow of rage and a crash and wild, terrified bleats as Freddie and Doris hurtled down the stairs, leaping like true mountain goats, with my father close behind, brandishing a fly whisk. 'I'll shoot them,' he screamed, and as the frightened animals dodged past him back up the stairs, he ran to the front hall where he kept his collection of bows and arrows. We cowered in a corner as he strung his most powerful Turkish bow and took two of the most lethal arrows off the wall. They had huge, sharp, vicious points. 'I'll get them, I'll shoot the bloody goats, out of my way!' We were now wailing with fright and even Bing had descended from her bedroom to see what all the fuss was about. 'Calm down, Duck,' she said, but her words fell on deaf ears. We heard him running up the stairs but there was no sign of the goats. 'Where are the bloody creatures?' he shouted. By chance Tessa, Hanks and Tod had caught up with them at the entrance to Tod's flat and were able to smuggle them down her back stairs to the old kitchen and so out the back door and round to Polly's stable where the door was firmly locked on them.

My father, grinding his teeth and stamping his feet, stood halfway up the stairs, the bow and one arrow poised in readiness. 'Come on, Ducky, be a good boy,' said my mother in an effort to calm him. 'Hanks is making you a goodly cup of coffee, she is bringing it to the library.' Bing turned on Kits and I, still quaking a step behind her: 'Oh, don't be so silly, feeble loons, go off and find Tod,' and my father swept past us, eyes narrowed, following Bing into the library and shutting the door. We escaped about as quickly as the goats had. My father recovered his composure fairly quickly, but we made sure that Freddie and Doris were kept out of his way for a considerable time.

In the autumn of 1947 Bing had to go to America, to New York, to appear as a witness in a court case involving her novel *Rebecca*. A case had been brought against her publishers, Doubleday's, and herself for plagiarism. It was not certain how long this case was going to take and her publisher, Nelson Doubleday, invited her to stay at his house on Long Island. My mother decided to take Kits and me along with her as well as Tod to give us our lessons. Tessa would be going to St Mary's, Wantage, in September, her first term at boarding-school.

Great activity took place at Mena preparing for these two events. Tessa spent hours sewing name-tapes on her school uniform, and Miss Tyrel, a local dressmaker, worked overtime making a complete wardrobe for my mother and one or two items for Tod and us children. Kits and I were now dressed alike in matching trousers and shirts and jerseys. I did not possess a dress or skirt and since Nanny left I had worn boys' clothes. Miss Tyrel made us matching blue wool trousers with bright red battledress jackets and several pairs of corduroys.

We all had new hairdos. Tessa had her lovely long plaits cut off and her first perm. When my father saw her new style he greatly offended her by roaring with laughter, saying, 'Good God, look at fairy flossy.' There was despair over my lank locks, until my father suggested that I have it cut in a Joan of Arc style. He was very keen on the French maiden and was forever reading books about her. The haircut was a great success and it was agreed that it made me look a little less plain.

At the beginning of September we all set off for London on the Cornish Riviera Express. At Par station Mr Allen, the stationmaster, was there to greet us, very smart in his morning-coat and top hat. Kits and I had to walk away down the platform because we got the giggles.

We had a compartment to ourselves. The journey seemed very long and I suffered from awful train sickness. Bing would make us go into the dining car for lunch, but I refused to eat anything. The dreadful bowls of swimming tomato soup which were plonked down was the end. At Paddington we were met by Maureen with two Godfrey Davies hire cars, one for us and one for the luggage. Kits and I felt sick on the way to Whitelands House and had to get out to walk the last bit.

My father's flat was on the sixth floor, looking out

over the Duke of York's headquarters and the King's Road. It was a dreary little flat with squeaky floorboards and no carpets. There were two small bedrooms, a sitting-room, a tiny kitchen and bathroom. It smelt faintly of gas and my father's eau-de-cologne. Tod had to take Kits and me to stay the night at the Sloane Square Hotel. My father took us all out to the Berkeley Buttery for supper. Kits and I were hopeless: we felt sick in the taxi going there and could scarcely eat anything, much to my father's annoyance: 'Bloody loons, can't take them anywhere.'

Maureen and my father came down in the train to Southampton to see us off on the *Queen Mary*. Kits and I were overcome with excitement this time. The *Queen Mary* was simply massive – a colossal floating hotel. We were overwhelmed by the sheer greatness of her, and we hung on to Tod, terrified that we would get lost.

We were shown to our cabins, two large staterooms. Tod and I were to share one and Bing and Kits the other. There were huge arrangements of flowers in both cabins, sent by friends and family. Tod made a thorough inspection of our cabin to make sure everything was clean. 'You never know who has been here before us,' she said. I thought the bathroom was wonderful with its small mahogany-sided tub and choice of fresh or salt water.

The voyage out was fairly calm, and Kits and I – 'the rotten sailors' – felt fine. Tod became a bit queasy, but Bing put it down to over-indulgence. Tod loved her food, and it was a tremendous treat to have such delicious meals after the dull Mena fare. Kits and I had to have our meals early with Tod in the vast dining-room, and this she resented for she liked meeting people. Bing sat at the Captain's table, but would rather have been with us.

We had great fun exploring all over the ship. We were taken on a tour of the engine-rooms, but the noise drove us out very quickly. We swam in the pool and played endless games with other children. Best of all, we enjoyed the deck with all the ping-pong tables. Bing would take us there and then go off for a walk with a friend called Pat Frier who happened to be on board.

Greta Garbo was a fellow passenger, and she would sometimes come and watch us play and even retrieve a ball or two if hit in her direction. She would sit in a deckchair with a rug over her knees, the collar of her camel coat turned up round her ears. We would show off, and make her roar with laughter when we galloped on all fours along the deck.

One day Kits and I got lost. We went to try to find Bing who had sauntered off while we were playing deck quoits. We found ourselves on a spacious staircase. We started going down and then couldn't find a way out, so we panicked and sat on the stairs and yelled. Seamen appeared from all directions and escorted us to the children's nursery. After what seemed like ages, Tod turned up with her cross face on and gave us a good ticking-off, which set me off again and it took all Bing's joking teasing to restore us.

Tod was decidedly grumpy with us on the *Queen Mary*. She kept muttering that she saw no 'folk', as she called the other passengers. We got rather fed up with her bad mood and one evening suggested that Tod should dine in Bing's place at the Captain's table. Tod, resplendent in a long black frock with green beading on the bodice and a jet necklace and earrings to match, sallied forth to the first-class dining-room. We were dreadful and, egged on by Bing, the three of us followed Tod at a discreet distance and watched her drinking cocktails and being introduced by Pat Frier to her fellow guests. Sad to say, giggles overcame us and we had to retire to our cabins. When she returned, flushed and slightly tipsy, all she could say was that she had not been 'very struck' by her fellow diners. 'Nothing to write home about,' she said as she heaved herself into bed. Her snores were really powerful that night.

On board the ship was Ellen Doubleday, the wife of Bing's American publisher. We met her for the first time a day or so into the voyage. She came into the stateroom one morning, a slim elegant woman, her arms filled with white flowers for Bing, and closely followed by a steward bearing a basket of splendidly wrapped gifts for us all. We were quite taken aback.

Bing was struck at once by Ellen's charm and beauty, and sat staring at the dark-haired vision before her. Ellen had seemed amused at the reaction and her large brown eyes had gazed back in some wonder. Even Tod was smitten by the allure of the quietly spoken American who arrived laden with goodly presents.

Ellen Doubleday took charge of us all from that moment on. She saw to it that Tod ate with the other passengers at the First Officer's table and that we joined some children in a young people's dining-room. She and my mother would walk a little along the decks but soon find long comfy chairs to sit in and converse for hours. Steaming bowls of chicken soup would be brought to them mid-morning and Kits and I would watch them, laughing and talking and we would play near by, showing off a little, hoping to catch Ellen's eye and be rewarded by her brilliant smile.

Sometimes Ellen would invite us into her large, bright stateroom. It smelt deliciously of her scent and she would let me look at her lovely evening dresses, wonderful silks and velvets. Bing and I were amazed by the variety of clothes in her cupboards. 'Ellen is always so smart, so well turned out,' Bing would say wistfully, and she would stare at herself in the looking-glass with a look of despondency which swiftly turned to wry amusement, when Ellen caught her eyeing the wardrobe. 'Daphne dear, please take anything you fancy, we are about the same size. I would love you to have one of my dresses,' Ellen told her.

Our arrival at New York was thrilling. Two vast cars, a Buick and a Cadillac, with smart, uniformed chauffeurs were there to meet us together with Nelson Doubleday's secretary. She travelled with Bing in the Buick, and we followed with Tod in the other car. Needless to say, Kits and I felt sick on the drive to Long Island. Barberrys was a lovely house, with terraces sloping down to beautiful gardens with wide sweeping lawns and spectacular views of Oyster Bay. It was the fall, and the trees were most splendid in their autumn tints. The house was very grand inside, with a gorgeous big drawing-room with magnificent furniture and big vases of flowers everywhere. Kits and I had a luxurious bedroom with pretty yellow and blue chintz curtains and bedcovers to match, as well as our own bathroom and dressing-room. Tod had the same next door to us, and Bing's room was white and pink with a four-poster bed.

It must have been a very worrying time for my mother. Her whole future as an author depended on the outcome of the lawsuit. Of course she had not copied a book by someone else called *Blind Windows*. It bore no resemblance to *Rebecca* except that the chief male character had been married before.

The Doubledays took tremendous trouble making us all feel welcome and at home. Life for Kits and me soon settled down into a routine. We would breakfast with

Tod in the small sunny breakfast-room and then begin
our lessons in the morning-room. This was used as a
study by Nelson Doubleday and he was kind enough
to lend it during our stay. Two sleek spaniels would
come and sit with us, staring in surprise at the intrud-
ers. At eleven Margaret, the smart, attractive house-
keeper, would come in with coffee and hot chocolate
and a large bowl of delicious apples. 'Fresh fruit from
the market, Miss Waddell,' she would say, smiling
brightly. We would race round the garden for ten
minutes and then get back to work until lunchtime.
This was taken with Tod in the breakfast-room. She
was very annoyed that she had to have this meal with
us, much preferring to eat with the Doubledays, and be
waited on in the large, grand dining-room. She did
have dinner with them and Bing, but it didn't stop her
grumbling about lunch. In the afternoons we would
take the dogs for a walk and then return to more
lessons.

My mother usually returned from New York as we
were finishing our tea, taken with Ellen Doubleday in
the drawing-room. Ellen would make Bing sit down
beside her on the sofa and tell her all about her day,
first making sure she had a cup of Earl Grey tea and a
piece of cinnamon toast. 'Not a word, Daphne dear,
until you have something warm inside you, no sir.' We
would catch Bing's eye and we would all have to look
away. We had a nickname for Ellen which was 'No sir',
for she said this often and Bing could imitate her
American accent, making us helpless with laughter.

Bing would tell us about her day in court, and usually
she was too exhausted by the time evening came to
want to do anything but have supper on a tray in her
room. Ellen then would have hers with her and sit
chatting, and Tod and Nelson sat in state in the dining-

room. At weekends there was often quite a lot of entertaining at Barberrys. Poor Bing dreaded this; she really did not want to meet people, being shy and always worried about having the right clothes. It was one of her main reasons for disliking London. She never thought she had the correct outfits, looking in despair at her reflection in the looking-glass. Ellen Doubleday also fussed Bing about her clothes and she had taken her off at the first opportunity to smart dress shops in and around New York. She wanted her husband's top-selling authoress to look good at the parties she gave for her.

Ellen was a very beautiful woman, dark and slim with wonderful velvet brown eyes. She was always dressed exquisitely, often changing three or four times a day. She had taken a dim view of Bing's wardrobe and so, apparently, had her lady's-maid, Tilly. On the evening of one of the first dinner parties we came into Bing's bedroom to say goodnight, to find her in quite a state. 'Guess what?' she said. 'Tilly thinks that my best evening dress is my nightgown, it really is the end,' and there, carefully laid out on the bed with bedjacket alongside, was Bing's beautiful white sharkskin dress. We stared in horror and then we all sank down to the floor, overcome with laughter. Tears poured down our faces. 'What the heck does Tilly think my nightdress is then?' wailed Bing. She stood up in the middle of the room, wondering whether she dared now wear the dress. She did, and looked stunning in it. Kits and I lay on her bed and marvelled at her loveliness and I wondered why she minded dressing up, for when she did she looked like a film star. I said how splendid she looked and she peered in the looking-glass uncon-vinced. 'I wish I could wear velvet trousers and a boyish belt,' she said.

We watched her go down the stairs. A few guests had already arrived and were standing about the hall. They stared at the slim, blonde figure coming towards them and we heard shouts of greeting, and soon she was surrounded by an admiring group.

Ellen was shocked to discover that I had no dresses or skirts. 'What are you doing to this child, Daphne?' she asked. 'She will grow up with no idea how to dress, got up like some little boy. I bet she is simply longing for some pretty things; we mustn't let her be a tomboy, no sir.' I was hauled off to Lord and Taylors in New York with Tod and Nelson's secretary, and bought dresses and skirts which I wore to please Ellen, but discarded once I had got back to Mena because Bing thought them 'too girlish and mincy'. She would mock me if I put any of them on: 'Oh, look at Bea, doesn't she look funny. You can't come for a walk like that – put your nice cords on, they suit you much better.'

CHAPTER TEN

One evening Noël Coward was among the guests at dinnner at Barberrys, and Kits and I were allowed down in our dressing-gowns for a short while during cocktails. Mr Coward made a great fuss of us, showing us tricks of throwing nuts into the air and catching them in our mouths. We, thoroughly overexcited, were eventually dragged from the drawing-room by Tod, resplendent in a long green brocade gown.

We were playing about on the floor of our bedroom when Kits was stung on the ankle by a sleepy wasp. He set up a howl and I dashed downstairs, but they had all gone to the dining-room and for a moment or two I stood in the doorway, awed by the sight of so many people seated along the large table with the candlelight flickering on their animated faces. Bing was next to Mr Coward and as I edged my way towards her I could see the latter had turned in his chair to face her, his back towards his other partner. He was smoking with a long cigarette-holder, the smoke curling up between them, and he was listening intently to what she was saying, eyebrows raised sharply. I sidled up to them and Bing looked at me in astonishment. I whispered what had happened and she glanced round the table anxiously for Tod. Mr Coward put his hand behind his ear and leant forward.

'What's amiss, you young thing?' he enquired. Bing told him and he immediately sprang to his feet. 'I'll come, I'll come,' he said, and he followed me up the stairs and found Kits rolling on the floor making a dreadful fuss. Mr Coward bent and picked him up, dropping him on the bed. 'Poor boy, poor boy,' he said very fast, and then crawled about on the floor looking for the wasp – which he found and beat into the carpet with the heel of his smart evening slipper. By this time the room had filled with onlookers and Tod, most put out by the interruption to her jolly evening, got hold of Margaret who produced a bottle of witch-hazel. Noël Coward came up twice more to see that 'the poor little chap was bearing up', and brought us goodies, candies wrapped up in his napkin. 'You'll live, you'll live,' he told Kits and blew us both a kiss.

One day in October we were having breakfast with Tod when, for some unknown reason, I said it was Polly's birthday. I had no idea when it really was, and I must just have said this for something to say. Tod, who had appeared that morning with one of her bad-mood faces on, cleared her throat and looked hard at me. 'Well,' she said, 'it happens to be mine.' We stared at her amazed and then felt very guilty for not knowing. Ellen had gone to New York with Bing so we couldn't let her know.

We were doing some reading in the morning-room after tea when Bing arrived back from her day at court. Somehow she had had time to shop and had bought us masses of toys and games. Tod's face got more and more 'hard chair' for there was nothing for her. I couldn't stand the atmosphere and at last said, 'Bing, you know it's Tod's birthday.' She had, of course, no idea. She was mortified and went immediately to Ellen who rose to the occasion and in no time a wonderful cake was produced and umpteen little presents, and Tod was toasted with champagne. Years later Tod and I always used to ring each other up on our birthdays and say in a solemn voice, 'It happens to be my birthday.'

Kits celebrated his seventh birthday on 3 November. This day was planned well in advance, and there were presents from everyone, and a splendid ice-cream cake in the shape of a red racing car. We were taken to a huge indoor rodeo, which we thought tremendous, and for days afterwards we bucked and reared on all fours, much to the amusement of Nelson Doubleday. Sometimes, just before our bedtime, he allowed us to watch the television in his dressing-room. We would sit on the end of his bed and watch a programme for children called *Small Fry*. We had never seen TV before and were mesmerised. He would sit with us, his large frame lying along the bed and his loud laughter would boom out and Ellen would come in dressed in her lovely house-coat prior to going to change for cocktails. She would tell him to keep the noise down.

Nelson was a big man, six foot four, with grey, wavy hair. He was not in the best of health – in fact I think he already was suffering from the cancer which was later to kill him, for I remember a doctor coming several times to give him injections in his bottom while we were there. He was always very friendly to Kits and me, and whenever he came across us he would beam and say in his loud clear voice, 'Well small fry, what goes on?'

As the court case wore on, Bing became very tired and thin. She was just forty years old, and the strain of those weeks took their toll. She became ill with nervous exhaustion and was made to go to bed and rest for some time. Ellen was a tower of strength. She looked after her and was a great support. We did not fully realise the seriousness of the case or how low Bing was feeling. We behaved badly a lot of the time, especially to Tod, playing her up too dreadfully. On one shopping spree I bought a life-size rubber rat and when Tod had gone down to dinner I slipped in to her room and put it in her bed. We tried to stay awake to hear the result but sleep overcame us.

The next morning, on our way down to breakfast, we peeped in to her room. In the waste-paper basket was the rat, or what was left of it, for it was cut into tiny pieces. Tod met us with a face like thunder and her bad mood lasted for several days. It was because of her moods that our behaviour worsened. At least mine did – poor Kits was led on. During our break in the mornings we would run out to the gardens and hide in the empty swimming pool. It was painted a lovely silver colour and it was great fun to slide down the side of the deep end. We would hear Tod calling us, and she would pass by, never thinking to look for us there. When she had gone we would dash back to the morning-room and be seated at the table when she returned, pink and breathless, and I would say, 'Tod, where have you been, we've been here for ages.'

To really upset her I would say that I thought that Bing had copied *Rebecca* from some other book, and poor Tod would go berserk: 'How could you, Flave, how could you say such an awful thing!' I was really horrid. Luckily Ellen had her wits about her and she overheard me one day being unkind. She called me

Menabilly as we first saw it

My mother transformed Menabilly

The Long Room at Menabilly

My mother spent many years of her youth at Ferryside

Kits and I were constant playmates

Above left: with Tod at Barberrys

Above: Kits, Tessa and me

Left: Kits and I sailing with my mother

My mother near the desk where she worked in her bedroom

Tessa became isolated as we grew older

Tessa aboard **Shimmer** *in Fowey harbour*

*Lord Louis Mountbatten
with my father*

My father with Margot Fonteyn

*Angela Halliday (Shaw)
with her two-seater MG*

*Carol Reed,
the film director*

My father became Comptroller of Princess Elizabeth's household

My father, Tessa and Aunt Grace at a cousin's wedding

My mother was inspired by Menab[*]

Tod, me, Kits and my mother

Peter Scott's drawings of Kits and me

My mother and father

Boating with my father

Ferryside

into her bedroom and showed me photos of her children, her daughters, Pucky and Neltje, and her son, Nelson. The latter was still very young and she told me how naughty he was. She gave me a long talking to and was very gentle and sweet. I felt so ashamed and swore to behave better and be nicer to Tod. She said that we would keep our chat a secret.

Thereafter Tod was very suspicious of my good behaviour. 'I can't make out what's got into Flave, she's a different being,' I overheard her saying to Ellen at tea-time.

'I guess she is growing up, and realises she can't be a thoughtless, silly child for ever, no sir.'

One weekend at Barberrys the Doubledays gave a large lunch party for Bing and, as their daughter Neltje would be home from school, Kits and I were invited with Tod. Neltje was thirteen, the same age as Tessa. She was tall and very slim with dark hair below her shoulders and wonderful deep, brown eyes, like Ellen's. Kits and I thought she was quite beautiful and Bing and Tod raved about her, saying that she made 'Tessa look as plain as Flave', and as unsophisticated. She wore striking, very grown-up clothes, and even nylon stockings which I thought were the height of glamour.

Thirty guests arrived for lunch and there was a long time spent over cocktails. Kits and I ran hither and thither handing out nuts and little eats. At lunch I'm afraid we disgraced ourselves. The first course was smoked salmon and we had never seen this delicacy before; one forkful was enough: clutching our mouths we rushed from the table and out on the lawn where we spat the salmon out on the grass. Tod was furious, shaking with rage. She marched us back and made us apologise to Ellen and Nelson Doubleday. He sat back and roared with laughter and waved us back to our seats. 'Come on, small fry, you'll just love what's coming next, chicken Maryland, get stuck into that.' Which we did and no one seemed to have noticed our behaviour, least of all Bing who was looking very pretty, surrounded by admirers.

Although Bing dreaded these parties, once she was there talking she looked as relaxed and calm as could be, joking and laughing, all the men's eyes on her; they flirted and she smiled and mocked them, which made them more interested.

Neltje was already dating boys, or beaux as she called them. They flocked around her and they would all go off in a fast red sports car to sail or play tennis. I thought of Tessa back home; the only boys she knew were John Burt who was a younger son of the Burts, and Guy Symondson, a great nephew of Lady Quiller-Couch. One holiday there had been a boy who had been rather keen, but we all mocked him and thought him so ugly and wet that Tessa cliffed him entirely. 'Cliff' was a family word for 'throwing out'. I thought I would have some good ammunition with which to bait poor Tessa when we returned home: 'What, no beaux?'

The middle of December arrived and with it the end of the horrid court case. Bing won the day and everyone was greatly relieved and thankful, but she was worn out. The Doubledays were very keen that we should spend Christmas with them, but Bing wished to return to Mena, my father and Tessa. So passages were booked once more on the *Queen Mary*, and Ellen and Nelson came to see us off.

The sleeping arrangements were as before, and I thanked my lucky stars that Tod and I were now on a much more friendly footing. When we arrived on board we found our cabins overflowing with flowers, many from Bing's fans and people that she had met while staying at Barberrys. There were vast bowls of fruit and many little gifts from Ellen, beautifully wrapped; Kits and I had one for each day of the voyage.

We were all sorry to say goodbye. The Doubledays had been so overwhelmingly generous and kind. Poor Tod was the saddest – she was dreading the cold of Mena after the warmth and comfort of Barberrys. We had lived in the lap of luxury, waited on hand and foot. Tod was determined to make the most of the crossing. Alas, a few hours out in the Atlantic we met with bad weather and we all remained in our bunks, sick as fifty cats for the entire journey. It was said to have been one of the worst crossings the ship had ever encountered. Tod suffered more than anyone. I can remember her saying as she lay groaning, 'Flave, darling, I wish I were dead.'

Bing was still suffering from her nervous exhaustion, and would have remained in bed in any case. At one point she got so fed up with Kits whining in the night that she handed him one of her sleeping-pills. She always took them, or at least had them handy, as she declared she was a rotten sleeper. If ever she left them behind when away she would have a 'white night'. Kits, in spite of sickness, was sharply on the ball. 'Are they for children?' he asked, and when told no was most offended to have been offered one.

The sea became calmer as we entered the English Channel, and Tod and I recovered enough to suddenly long for some food for we had not eaten for four days. It was about five in the evening when Tod declared she thought a little bit of thinly cut brown bread and butter would not go amiss, and perhaps some chicken soup. We rang for the steward.

He arrived and before we could place our order he started to strip off his clothes. 'Young man, what do you think you are doing?' cried the outraged Tod. The man was now down to his underpants and he paraded in front of us, saying, 'I thought you might like to see the bruises I incurred during this rough passage.' He was indeed black and blue and I sat up, very interested, watching him turn about, feeling better by the minute. He had awful purple marks on his thighs. 'Put your clothes on at once or I shall report you to the Captain.' Tod's illness was all forgotten as she struggled to sit up and take command.

Our first bite of food after so long was utter bliss. We sat on our bunks feeling quite merry and went next door to fetch Kits, but Bing looked very white and wretched and refused to have anything to eat: 'I really couldn't, just can't face it.' The next morning Tod became anxious and got the ship's doctor to her side, but he only declared that it was indeed exhaustion. We were able to get up and have meals for the first time in the dining-room while Bing remained in her bunk.

Tod and I were in despair over my hair. During the last few days I had not given it a comb or brush and the result was an awful tangled mess. It was completely matted. 'Flave, darling, it's beyond a joke, you will have to have it cut,' said Tod. So off we went to the children's hairdresser where I was given an urchin cut. Tod had gone off while it was being done and hadn't heard my instructions. 'I would like to look like a boy, please,' I had said. She was horrified when she saw the results and dragged me back to Bing who, lying listless in bed, longed to be left alone. She did smile when she saw me, though: 'Oh, that's lovely, you should have had that done months ago,' and we looked at each other, a kind of secret knowledge passing between us, the longing to be boyish. Tod crumbled whenever she looked at me, saying that any looks I might have had had quite vanished. 'You look for all the world like the Artful Dodger in *Oliver Twist*,' she said sadly.

Maureen was at Southampton to meet us and we all travelled back in the boat-train to London. At Whitelands House Bing collapsed into bed and the doctor was called. He said she was to have complete rest and quiet. The excitement of coming home was marred by her illness and her feeling so down. Tod went off to stay with a friend and my father cooked us delicious scrambled eggs for our supper. Kits and I shared the little spare room.

CHAPTER ELEVEN

Tod, Kits and I returned to Cornwall two days later after a magical visit to Bertram Mills Circus at Olympia with my father and Maureen. After the performance we were taken to see the animals and I went mad over the beautiful liberty horses, a string of matching chestnuts with tall plumes in their manes. Mr Mills himself took us round and we were given a delicious tea. Then Maureen took us to the funfair which was thrilling. She had great trouble getting us off the roundabout – ride after ride we had – and Kits went wild on the dodgems and had to be forcibly removed. We ate candy floss until it was coming out of our ears and, needless to say, felt queasy on the car journey back to the flat.

Bing was very unwell until Christmas, though was able to pull herself together in time to decorate the house. Mena really came into its own at Christmas. Bing ventured out in the woods and hacked off great branches of fir and holly, threading them through the banisters. She draped long, trailing pieces behind pictures, wall lights and looking-glasses. In the front hall a large red paper bell hung from the ceiling which Kits and I vainly tried to jump up and touch. Our nursery was dressed overall with gaudy paper chains left over from Nanny's day. There was a general air of excitement, rising to fever pitch on Christmas Eve.

On Christmas morning Kits and I woke at five and opened our stockings. We never believed in Father Christmas as Bing thought it all wrong to tell children such lies. She had never got over the disappointment as a child of being told by older children that he did not exist. We were too excited to eat breakfast and waited impatiently for the breakfast trays to go to Bing's bedroom. We passed the time by going to wish Tessa happy Christmas and to see what she had in her stocking. Then the three of us ran along to Bing. My father was sitting up in bed eating his boiled egg, glasses on the end of his nose and glancing at the latest yachting magazine, and Bing was sipping coffee with a smile on her face. We all exchanged kisses, and were given token presents, our main ones to be opened at the tree after tea.

Gran, the two girls and our Great-Aunt Billy, Gran's elder sister, arrived in time for drinks before lunch. They brought with them Gran's closest friend, Kate Loder, a favourite of ours, who had a way of telling very funny stories. Another friend of the family, Angela Halliday, six-foot tall and nicknamed 'Shaw', also arrived with them. The dining-room table was gloriously decorated by Bing and Tod with pyramids of crackers in front of each plate. The twenty-pound turkey, cooked to perfection by Mrs Burt, was carried in by my father who staggered a little under the weight. My father began to carve, aiming a discreet kick at the visiting Pekes. He made a tremendous fuss of lighting the Christmas pudding, pouring far too much brandy over the top and making Gran exclaim that we would all be tipsy. Then came the best part, the cracker-pulling. Kits and I usually cheated, holding the cracker so far up that we were sure of getting the prize. We watched with glee while Gran fitted a paper hat on her head. She was vain and got out her powder compact to make adjustments, putting the hat at a more flattering angle. If she decided the hat didn't suit her, she would look about her for more suitable attire, her mouth pulled down in disdain at Bing who always appeared ravishing though she couldn't have cared less. Kits and I would have to dive under the table to hide our giggles. This was an error, though, because the ankle-biting Pekes were lurking, ready to pounce. They were already on the warpath having drawn blood after Tod had pushed them roughly out of the way with her 'Allez, allez'.

The conversation at lunch was about our trip to the States and the horrid court case. Gran made sort of moaning sounds, saying, 'I shouldn't have known what to do, poor Daphne, how absolutely beastly.' She became very downcast and her sister Billy said, 'Ach, ach,' her full cheeks trembling with emotion. They cheered up when Noël Coward was mentioned, adding further tales about him concerning the time he had visited the du Maurier family in Hampstead.

After lunch Bing tried to make everyone go for a walk, but there was open rebellion. We little ones had already walked across the park in the morning with Tod to Tregaminnion church. It had been very chilly, with a few people there, and the usual mousetraps on the altar steps had put paid to Tod making her Communion. My mother never went to church. She disliked public worship, preferring to say her prayers in private rather than surrounded by other people. My father loved Fowey church and took Tessa with him. He was proud of her good looks and liked her with him.

At long last, after a tea of rich Christmas cake and mince-pies, we were summoned to the Long Room. We had been banned from the room for the last twenty-four hours while my father had decorated the tree. He even went as far as drawing all the curtains so that we wouldn't peep. Now as we stood waiting to be admitted, even the grown-ups talked excitedly, pushing each other in the hall. The door was flung open and we were transported into a fairy land. The long room was in darkness, but at the far end of the room the magnificent tree glowed and shimmered with a thousand twinkling lights. We all advanced further into the room, our eyes as round as saucers, and everyone let out breathless 'oohs' and 'aahs'.

The candles flickered and shone and all the coloured balls and bright hanging tinsel objects glistened and gleamed. There was a light dusting of frost over the branches and on the very top a gold star glowed warmly. Underneath the tree presents were piled, some bedecked in ribbons, some with beautifully tied bows. We could always tell the ones that Bing had wrapped for the paper was puckered and somewhat bedraggled with the ribbons askew. We were allotted places to sit and Bing crawled about on the floor, ready to hand out the gifts. Kits and I were runners and handed the goodies to each person in turn while my father stood by his masterpiece, keeping a watchful eye on the candles to see they did not burn too fiercely. There was much rustling of paper and repeated 'oohs' and 'aahs' as presents were received with delight.

That year, we all, every Jack man of us, gave Great-Aunt Billy soap: soap, sponges and flannels. As these goods piled up around her, she became ruffled, darting looks hither and yon. Her little griffon dog, Spitfire, perched on her knee, took on its owner's mood and glared round in a suspicious manner. Suddenly we were all startled by Billy exclaiming loudly, 'Ach, ach.' The *pièce de résistance* was a scrubbing-brush, hand-painted and meant for Spitfire's daily grooming. This was the final insult. Billy stood up, Spitfire trembling in her arms, and, muttering loud 'Naas, nass' sounds, stalked from the room, her Black Watch kilt swinging merrily. She spent the rest of the 'tree' in the library talking to her dog on a very 'hard chair'.

It took all my father's considerable charm to placate Aunt Billy, explaining what a coincidence it was that we should all have given her washing things, and of course it didn't mean that we thought she never bathed. He took her arm and led her back to the fold, pointing out the funny side, and in a short time she was sitting down, tears pouring down her cheeks with laughter while the champagne poured down her throat.

After all the visitors had departed, Bing collected her presents and went to her room to lie down. She was still suffering from the weakness that her illness had brought upon her, and she said her head ached with coping with the two families. Kits crept up with her, and together they curled up in bed, both exhausted by their day.

My father's good mood lasted until the champagne ran out and then he made himself a stiff gin and lime. This turned him testy, and we had learnt to steer clear of him then. He dropped all his presents on the floor, gave them a hearty kick and swore at anyone left in sight. Tod, Tessa and I beat a hasty retreat to her flat where Tod concocted some delicious soup from the turkey stock, and we sat in her kitchen drinking this goodly broth, picking over the day's events.

Apart from the excitement of Christmas we had little else in our lives in the way of treats. We did, on the other hand, have one enormous dread: a visit to the dentist. We were never told about such visits until the actual day of the appointment. Lunch would be slightly earlier than usual and we knew then that we were for it. To this day I have a sinking feeling at the very thought of sitting in the dentist's chair. At two o'clock sharp Tod would stand out on the gravel sweep, dressed in a neat blue suit, her face set, standing no nonsense, waiting for Mr Gill and his taxi. We would hang back, standing about in the library, hoping against hope that Mr Gill would have forgotten or his car would break down. We irritated Bing by our moans and groans for, in point of fact, Kits had a perfect set of teeth and had never had to have a filling. It was me who worked him up.

Mr Gill had two ambitions in life: to be a racing driver and to go to Tasmania. We could hear the car coming all the way from the top park gate. It would roar up the little hill to the front door and slide to a stop, inches from Tod. Mr Gill was small and swarthy with well-brilliantined dark hair. He had a slightly gypsy look. The car was a supercharged Vanguard, the terror of the roads. Tod would get in the back with me beside her, and Kits in the front with Mr Gill. We would speed across the park, charging through the deep potholes, Tod tutting loudly. Once on the main road, Mr Gill could not stand being overtaken by other cars. If he saw a threat in his mirror, his foot would go down on the accelerator and the car would surge forward. He would then turn round in his seat and grin at us in the back. Tod would shut her eyes and clasp her bag even more firmly. There was a certain stretch of road across Par Moor which was straight and true. Here Mr Gill could, if conditions were favourable, reach a dizzy seventy miles an hour. He once overtook our doctor on this road: 'Left him standing, I did!' he told us with glee.

Arriving at the dentist Kits and I would toss a coin to decide who was to go first. Mr Foster would greet us with a wide grin on his face, showing rather yellow teeth. I was no sooner in the chair when he would reach for the dreaded drill, and my heart would sink. I must have had shocking teeth because they always needed filling and I had a plate by now that had to be adjusted. Mr Foster always hurt, and by the time I left the room I was quite weak with pain and nerves. Poor Mr Foster eventually got his comeuppance. We heard years later that he went on safari in Africa after he retired and was eaten by a crocodile. I have no idea how true this story is, but the thought of all those teeth doing for him makes one wonder.

As a treat after our ordeal Tod would head for the bakery on the corner opposite the dentist. It was the most wonderful cake shop and appealed to Tod's sweet tooth. We would select sickly buns and sink newly filled teeth into them. Looking back, I suspect Mr Foster observed us from his window with glee, his hand straying towards the drill. We would also visit W.H. Smith's and be allowed to put something down on Bing's account, usually dinky toys for Kits and an Enid Blyton book for me. Mr Gill would be waiting for us, a little redder in the face, champing to be off. The home journey was even more hairy than the outward one for, having got over our ordeal, we would egg Mr Gill on. Tod and I would be thrown about like rag-dolls in the back while Kits up front, his face bright with mischief, would warn Mr Gill of any enemy car about to overtake. At the park gates, if the weather was fine, Tod would insist on walking – enough was enough.

My father decided it was time I learnt to ride properly. He said I looked like a sack of potatoes on Polly. Mr Burt knew of a riding school on the road to Truro, so I started at Miss Stocker's of Sticker. She was a thin, dark woman and very bossy. I was put on board a very skittish pony called Peter and made to go round and round a large field to show her what, if anything, I could do. I could not rise to the trot and Peter bolted with me and we galloped out of control until he tired himself out. 'We'll have to do better than that, Miss,' said Miss Stocker. Every Thursday afternoon I was driven to Sticker and was given lessons by either Miss Stocker or her young assistant, a man called Richard. I rode Peter or a seventeen-hand horse called Cromwell. He was kind and gentle and extremely comfortable. I learnt to jump on him and did so well that Miss Stocker promised to take me hunting. Bing, of course, was very 'Mrs Brown' at the notion. My father thought it was a good idea, though. 'Let the Old Gump have a go,' he said.

I was getting too big for Polly now, but I still rode her every day. We would charge rather recklessly through the woods and across the park. One afternoon she was tethered on the side lawn peacefully grazing when I gave her a small piece of bread. She started to choke and cough. This went on for about half an hour and, as she was obviously in some distress, we rang the vet. The long and the short of it was that she had done something to her windpipe. The vet said that she must never be ridden beyond a walk again. Poor Polly, I was heartbroken. She was retired out to grass with an old riding hack of the farmer's, Tommy Dunn, down at Menabilly Barton farm. Polly lived until she was twenty-six, and was happy to the end.

My father proved a great ally when I approached

Bing about getting another pony. 'Something with a bit of go, about fourteen hands,' he said. Mr Burt proved useful once again. He got word of three ponies for sale out St Austell way. On a Saturday morning my father agreed to take me off to view the animals. We set forth in the old Ford. I wore my best cords and carried my riding-crop, a much prized possession with my initials engraved in silver, a gift from my godfather, Augustus Agar.

My father's knowledge of Cornwall was very good, but alas, we were soon lost. His jovial mood on setting out was turning nasty. As usual he was chain-smoking and starting to click his tongue against his teeth, a sure sign of irritation. When we went in the wrong direction for the fourth time he began grinding his teeth. I was red in the face and feeling sick. By some fluke we hit the right road and found the right farm. We were met by a nervous man and his small daughter. My father's face did not inspire confidence. 'Well, where is the creature?' he barked, lighting his umpteenth cigarette. Round the corner came a truly pretty little pony, chestnut with four white socks. But alas, only eleven hands.

'What's that?' my father asked.

The man jumped and couldn't speak.

'How lovely,' I said politely.

'He's very nippy,' replied the small girl.

'He'll have to be to get out of my way,' said my father very rudely, and stalked back to the car. We backed out of the yard as fast as the Keystone Cops and drove somewhat jerkily up the road, smoke pouring from my father like some demented dragon. We stopped for directions, and came to the next victim. My father refused to get out of the car. 'Go on, don't be an arse, go and ring the doorbell,' he said, and I went up the garden path to the front door of a shambling old house with dirty windows. A strange old lady opened the door. I asked for Mr Pierce.

'Gone out in the lorry,' she said flatly.

'We have come to see the pony,' I said.

'He's taken it in the lorry,' she replied and shut the door.

I reported back to my father who snorted with disgust. 'I will buy the next one,' I said, near to tears.

'Don't be so bloody silly, it will most likely be a cart-horse,' he snapped.

At the end of a muddy lane we arrived at our last appointment, again a farm, though large and well kept. Father, daughter and son met us plus a very pretty blonde mother. My father changed gear immediately on shaking hands with her and was charm itself. We all sat and talked in the rambling sitting-room with large cups of coffee. I soon became restless to see the pony.

'Go and saddle Joey up,' said the father and we all trooped out to a field beyond the house. Tied to the gate was a stocky pony of about fourteen hands. I heard my father mutter, 'Christ.'

Joey was very, very plain. He had a large Roman nose, a hogged mane, and someone had started to trace-clip him giving up midway, resulting in a queer, moth-eaten appearance. He had a bridle on top of a halter and was covered in mud. My father inhaled deeply and narrowed his eyes.

'Can I try him, please,' I said in desperation. I was duly hoisted into the saddle and I steered him into the field. We trotted and trotted, going faster and faster until we were fairly flying along. But would he canter or gallop? Not a hope. By this time I had a roaring stitch and was quite breathless.

'Kick on, kick on! barked my father, to no avail. I

pulled up before the little group. 'Well, that was pretty hopeless,' my father said.

'He goes very nicely once he knows you,' said the son.

'I am sure he does,' I replied, and to my father said that he was just what I was looking for.

'Are you mad?' he said, and with his hands in his pockets turned to make his goodbyes.

'Please, Daddy,' I said. 'I really want him,' and I did.

He stood looking at me in amazement. 'Well, you're easily pleased,' he said, and very reluctantly handed over twenty pounds cash.

'God, what an exhausting morning,' he said as we drove back. 'Darling, are you really sure about that ugly brute?' I promised I was. When we returned to Mena he made hasty tracks to the sideboard for a large gin and lime.

CHAPTER TWELVE

Captain Vanderleur was the agent for the Menabilly estate. He lived in the grounds in a large wooden shack overlooking some fields with a wonderful view of the sea and Gribbin Head. He lived alone except for two mongrel dogs called Ruffy and Trudy. He was in charge of the maintenance of the woods and paths and the walled garden, and kept an eye on the farm and the tiny village of Hamlin and any other parts of land not let to Bing. There was a splendid camellia plantation to the right of Polly's field with some rare and fine specimens. These were Captain Vanderleur's pride and joy and were strictly out of bounds. Bing was particularly fond of camellias and there were very few in her part of the garden. At times she got the urge to have a vase or two in the house. There were twenty-eight vases to be filled with flowers every week or so, and the thought of camellias were very tempting.

Kits and I would ride our bikes up to the look-out, the narrow road that went past the Captain's house, to see if his car was in the garage, and then report back to Bing. If all clear, she would saunter across the lawn, secateurs in her pocket and, with Kits and I keeping cavey, creep into the plantation. It was a Garden of Eden, with camellias of every size and colour – great splashes of scarlet, clouds of dazzling white and the softest pink. Even we children were enchanted. Once in the Holy of Holies, Bing darted from tree to tree, cutting as much as she dared without fear that an eagle eye would spot the loss. Then quickly back across the lawn with Kits and I like outriders, guarding her on either side. The Captain did once catch her red-handed. She stepped out of the bushes practically into his arms, and then tried to hide the flowers behind her back. 'Good evening, how nice to see you,' he said. 'Do please let me know if you would ever like some camellias as I should be most happy to give you a flower or two.' Poor Bing, scarlet with shame, backed away from him as if he were royalty.

Kits and I once stole some apples from his orchard down at the walled garden. Tod was furious with us and made us go and apologise. We rode our bikes slowly up to his shack. Trees grew round it, and only the wide veranda in the front was open. He was sitting, an oil-lamp at his feet, staring out to sea, a pair of captured German field glasses on his lap. He asked us in, and Trudy and Ruffy sniffed at our shoes, making low growling noises. Captain Vanderleur looked like a tall, thin toad. He was dressed in brown cords and jacket with a sort of Dutch bargeman's peaked cap. His pale brown eyes would glide over you, and he had a way of darting the tip of his tongue out of his mouth. We confessed to pinching the apples and he stared toad-like at us. He was a JP and we were terrified he would give us some awful punishment. To our astonishment he let out a bellow of laughter which made the dogs bark loudly. 'Help yourselves whenever you like,' he said, and took us into the house and handed us a large basket of cookers to give to Bing. We were very intrigued by his sitting-room, crowded with strange Eastern sculptures and rickety bamboo furniture.

He saw us looking about and seemed amused. 'I lived in India when I was young,' he said, 'wonderful country, might go back one day.' We waited politely to be shown out, but he was in no hurry. He smiled down at Kits. 'I have a small house on Bodmin Moor. Perhaps you would like to come up there some time and stay for a day or so.'

Kits moved closer to me and said, 'Our mother doesn't like us going away on our own.'

'You ought to join the Boy Scouts,' said the Captain. 'I take a troop camping in the summer on the moors, they love it.'

Kits took my hand and looked at his feet. 'Thank you for the apples. We must go now,' I said, and we were let out and fled back on our bikes.

Tod was very cross that we had got away scot-free and been given more apples. 'Well, count yourselves lucky,' she said.

Captain Vanderleur was truly angry with all of us when Carol Reed, the film director, came to stay. Carol had been a boyfriend of Bing's when they were both very young and starting out on their careers. They had remained great friends.

We had just finished dinner when Carol suddenly said, 'Let's have a bonfire, I really feel like having a huge bonfire.'

We fell about laughing. 'Don't be silly, Carol, it's dark and we have nothing to burn,' said Bing.

'Yes, we have,' said Carol, 'that huge rhododendron bush at the end of the pony's field by your writing hut. You said yourself its height spoils the view of the sea. We'll burn that, it'll make a marvellous fire. Come on, everyone. We need paper, paraffin, matches and another glass of wine to light us up.'

In no time we were all tearing across the lawn, eager and excited. The rhododendron was at least thirty feet high and about twenty feet wide. Carol disappeared in the depths of the bush and poured liberal amounts of paraffin on all the branches in sight. He put armfuls of newspapers between the lower branches and told us all to stand well clear. 'I am now going to put the first match to my handiwork,' he shouted. We stood still, holding our breath. We waited for some time and then a small glow appeared through the leaves and Carol came running out, his face streaked with dirt, but with a huge grin from ear to ear. There was a great whoosh and the whole bush caught fire. Sparks flew out and the heat soon became intense.

We danced about in glee as flames shot high into the air, lighting up the sky. It must have been seen from miles around for the Rowe family living at the wall gardens came rushing to see what it was, and the Duns from the farm. We were quite a gathering. 'We thought 'twas the blinking house on fire, like in the film, *Rebecca*,' someone said. They had all become acquainted with the movie.

Captain Vanderleur, sitting peacefully on his veranda, saw the red glow in the sky and thought his beloved plantation was on fire. He charged down the path from the look-out, dogs snapping at his heels. He could not believe his eyes. He strode over to the admiring audience and shouted at Bing, his voice high-pitched above the noise: 'What on earth do you think you are doing? How did this rhododendron catch fire?'

'Hello there, isn't this fun?' shouted back Carol. 'We thought it was just the night for a good blaze. Jolly good, you're here in time, have a glass of wine.'

The Captain stared in amazement at Carol and the fire. He swallowed several times, rage threatening to engulf him. 'Do you mean you deliberately started this fire, wantonly setting it alight?'

He moved towards Carol who laughed brightly. 'Absolutely right, old chap, horrible old bush, poor Daph couldn't see the sea from her bedroom window, she'll have no problem now.' He put his arm round Bing who was trying to hide behind him.

Captain Vanderleur blinked and his dogs prowled round his feet growling. 'You will be hearing from the Estate, Mrs Browning, and no doubt Dr Rashleigh. This is very serious indeed.' And with a withering look he departed, dogs bounding after him.

The locals had melted away into the night as soon as they had heard the Captain's tone; they didn't want to be involved. Poor Bing started back towards the house, but Carol dragged her back: 'Silly old spoilsport. What's it to do with him? It's your land.' But Bing explained that it wasn't really hers and that she had strict rules to abide by where the grounds were concerned. She did indeed get letters from the Captain warning her about her rights, but luckily not from Dr Rashleigh.

A very nice boy called Jimmy Husband used to come and ride Joey with me. His father occasionally helped Mr Burt in the garden and they lived up in Hamlin village. Jimmy was fifteen and good-looking, dark with lovely green eyes. We would spend hours grooming the pony and cleaning tack and then building jumping lanes in the Cedar Walk. I was still very much the tomboy and Jimmy was shy and rather quiet, so any boy/girl relationship never entered our heads. Tod thought otherwise, though; she would stalk us and appear suddenly as if by magic.

One day she took me to see *Wuthering Heights* at the Fowey cinema and it was after this film that Tod became obsessed; at meal-times she would quiz me and complain to Bing, saying, 'My dear, if we don't watch out it will be a case of Cathy and Heathcliff all over again.' But Bing would hoot with laughter: 'Don't be silly, Tod, Fave is only eleven and no oil painting, and poor Jimmy isn't interested in that sort of thing,' and she would dismiss the conversation much to Tod's fury and my 'hard chair' at being so described.

Bing told us all the facts of life when we were very young. Kits and I cannot remember ever not knowing. She explained about menstruation, which the family nicknamed 'Robert'. She said it was most important for men to know as it would help them understand their womenfolk better in later life. I was glad she did because one morning, waking in our bedroom, I leapt out of bed to be met with cries of 'Robert, Robert, Beaver, you've got Robert!', and glancing down I saw to my horror that my white silk pyjamas (cast-offs belonging to my mother's friend Gertrude Lawrence) were soaked in blood. Kits took me by the hand and rushed me to Bing who was having her bath.

'Oh, you poor thing,' she cried and I promptly fainted on the floor. I was sent to bed for two days and Kits waited on me hand and foot, and each month made sure that I knew when I was due, keeping a note of dates. The worst part was Bing saying that now I was no longer really boyish, but just a boring old girl and said I looked even plainer when I had it which was fairly dooming of her.

In 1948, my father resigned from the army. In the beginning of that year he became Comptroller to HRH Princess Elizabeth and the Duke of Edinburgh's Household. He helped to establish them in Clarence House. My father took great pride in his job and loved every moment of his work. He continued to live in Whitelands House off the King's Road during the week and Bing, anxious to support him in his new job, went up to London more frequently to attend royal functions and other social events. She disliked London and would return to the peace and quiet of Mena, thankful to be back in her own 'Roots'. 'I shouldn't mind if I never saw London again,' she often said. They both had many friends living there, and would occasionally invite the odd one to stay, but Bing was always worried that people would find Mena too shabby, the food not good enough. In fact, the food had much improved. Mrs Burt came almost daily and was an excellent cook. In addition, a very nice girl called Gladys who lived nearby came to help in the house with cleaning; she could cook as well which was a great blessing.

Bing got into a tremendous panic when Ellen Doubleday wrote to ask if she could come and stay for a few days in the summer. Thinking of the superb food at Barberrys and the wonderful service, Bing nearly lost her head. 'What are we to do? There is no proper spare room,' she cried. Tod rose to the occasion and organised a total decorating scheme for the Blue Lady room, and went as far as putting in a bathroom en suite. Once finished, the new bedroom looked lovely with its thick white carpet, red, white and blue chintz curtains bordered with a smart twisted-rope effect, and new twin beds. King's Road was raided for choice bits of furniture and pictures. Kits and I were amazed by the transformation and used to sneak in and sit and admire the room, sometimes having a quick dive on to the new beds, careful to tidy the bedcovers afterwards.

Tod said the room was good enough for royalty and we detected a certain gleam in my father's eye at the suggestion. She put Bing at ease by saying she would supervise the cooking, plan the meals and cook the dinners herself. This she did and caused havoc in the kitchen, sending Mrs Burt and Gladys nearly mad.

Ellen arrived in May when Mena was looking its best. The rhododendrons were beautiful and the twenty-eight vases scattered about inside were filled with the Captain's camellias. Bing's new worry was that my father and Ellen would not get on, but this was needless. All went well; Ellen fell in love with Mena and succumbed to my father's boyish charm. He flirted, twirling his moustache, and waited on her hand and foot.

Tod's food was delicious though somewhat rich. 'What's old Tod going to dish up now, some muck with a sickly sauce?' we heard my father mutter prior to dinner. Ellen would appear down from her room in a long black chiffon dress with soft ruffles at her neck and wrists, pearls gleaming against her white throat. She would glide into the drawing-room and look Bing up and down, resplendent in her pretty house-coat, a gift from New York. My father would hand Ellen a mammoth dry Martini, his green eyes dancing with good spirits, and Ellen, appreciative of everything, would sit holding forth about friends back on Long Island and would down two more Martinis before Tod, flushed and flustered, would announce 'The food is in.'

Ellen would help herself to a generous portion, exclaiming how good it all looked, and leave almost everything on her plate. She would eat about four mouthfuls and then put down her fork. The first time this happened Bing and Tod were in a fever, thinking the fish was off, but as it happened at every meal they realised it must be some little quirk. My father said it was because she was awash with dry Martinis.

My mother was disappointed that Ellen did not want to walk more. She longed to take her about Mena. 'I'm not going to trundle round those woods, Daphne, no sir,' Ellen would say. 'What's wrong with sitting right here in the drawing-room and having a good chat?' Poor Bing was forced to sit indoors on a glorious spring day, while Ellen droned on, chain-smoking like my father. Eventually she would fall asleep mid-sentence with her mouth wide open, and Bing would sneak out for a welcome breath of air.

Ellen had brought some of her cast-off clothes for Bing. Miss Tyrel came to do the alterations, but most of the outfits were very smart, more suitable for London or some royal do, and Bing lost interest in them. Luckily Maureen made sure they were taken up to Whitelands House for future wear. Ellen was quite staggered by our lack of social life. She couldn't understand why Bing did not want to entertain guests every weekend. 'Have a few girls for lunch,' she would say. 'Doesn't Tommy want his menfolk about him?' Bing had replied that it was their one idea of hell having 'folk' around them. 'I couldn't write or think,' she explained.

'Do the children never meet others of their own age?' Ellen asked. 'Why, Daphne, it is not civilised, you've gotta do something about it, yes sir.' And where were Tessa's beaux? It hardly bore thinking of. Bing looked vague and said she didn't really know anyone much except for a few cronies at the yacht club, and anyway she would simply hate to have to visit other people's houses; we loved Mena. Ellen had given her a withering look and had tried the same tactics with my father. That too fell on deaf ears.

So when a few weeks later some friends of Angela Halliday (Shaw) rang up with an invitation, Bing seized the moment. 'Put the kids into their best party frocks,' she was told, 'and send them down; we'll give them a whale of a time.' Gillian Carlyon lived with her mother in a lovely house near St Blazey called Tregrehan, known to the locals as 'Hangover Hall', for Mrs Carlyon was fond of a drop of the hard stuff. Gillian grew the finest camellias in the country. We had never been invited to the house before and were all for refusing but Bing, with Ellen's words ringing in her ears, had accepted, saying we would love to go.

There was total panic. We had no party clothes – I hadn't even got a single dress I could fit into now that Nanny had left. Tessa only had her school uniform and sailing kit. All my jeans were dirty or at any rate stained with garlic marks. Bing said we would have to rifle her cupboards and she threw open the doors, looking in despair at what lay within. Tessa found a blue silk cocktail dress of Ellen's, rather more suitable for high-balls in a Manhattan penthouse than a children's party, and it looked decidedly odd with school sandals.

The best I could come up with was a thin tweed skirt, far too hot, which came to my ankles, and a shiny black T-shirt with big white initials E D in satin on the bosom. This had shrunk in the wash and fitted snugly, like a glove. Kits lent me some new white cricket socks, rather warm and on the small side, and I found a pair of quite presentable black plimsolls. Tod had to sew me into the skirt to prevent it slipping to the floor. 'It's a disgrace, Flavè, darling, you have no dress to wear,' she said. Kits gave me a very dubious look and said I looked like Old Mother Riley. He was fine, got up in shorts and a clean shirt.

Shaw came to collect us in her two-seater MG. She usually wore trousers but today she wore a smart linen dress. She looked us up and down. 'Your mother should be in the doghouse,' she said. 'Why can't she buy you some decent clothes?' She said I looked as if I was wearing a hearth rug. With these words of comfort we squashed into the MG. Shaw was six-foot tall, and how she managed to fit behind the steering wheel was a mystery. We had to have the canvas roof down to get us three in.

Tregrehan seemed much grander than Mena and we gasped at the wonderful hall and wide staircase. There were children running in all directions, shouting and laughing and all dressed in proper frilly party dresses, the boys in pale linen shorts and ruffled shirts. Many of them stopped their dashing around and came and stared at us. We stood as near to Shaw as we could and longed for the floor to swallow us up. We heard faint titters and one small voice was heard asking, 'Is it a fancy dress party? Can I dress up?' We did not wait to hear the answer for Shaw marched us off to find our hosts.

We found ourselves in a room with walls covered in shelves of leather-bound books and most of the chairs piled high with catalogues on gardening. Two French bulldogs rushed at us and licked our feet and hands. Gillian came up and said hello. I was pleased to see she was wearing none too clean jeans. 'Go and join the other kids, the library is for grown-ups.' A tall, fair-haired man came up and started talking to Shaw. We had not budged from our stand by the door. Shaw introduced us to the man. 'This is Noël Langley, he is a film director,' she said. We shook hands. Tessa asked him if he knew Carol Reed. He said of course he did and wandered off. Mrs Carlyon came puffing into the room. She was also wearing rather grubby trousers. She waved vaguely in our direction. A herd of children followed her into the room and she rounded on them, clapping her hands loudly: 'Shut up all of you and come and have tea.' She had to shout above the din. A wild shriek went up and the throng surged out of the library and raced off in search of food.

In the dining-room there was a fight to be seated at the table. There were about twenty children in all and Mrs Carlyon must have underestimated the amount of guests she had invited for there were not enough chairs or plates to go round or, so it would seem, tea. We all sat and ate in a sort of rota system. A sandwich, biscuit and half a piece of cake was put on a plate in front of us and scarcely had we time to finish when the plate was snatched from under our noses, wiped on the back of Mrs Carlyon's trousers, and plonked in front of someone else. The half-dozen grown-ups went without eats, but were permitted a cup of tea. We were given watery orange juice. As tea was by far my favourite meal I took a dim view of this carry-on.

'As soon as you have finished your tea, please get down and go out in the garden out of the way,' Gillian shouted at the gathering. When we were shoved out in the garden there were heated arguments as to what games should be played. No two children could agree so we three wandered off to have a good snoop round. I had to walk rather like a hobbled horse for the tweed skirt was very narrow, and in the end I dragged it up round my hips in an ungainly bunch and held it with one hand. We explored the stable complex and admired an attractive fountain in a walled part of the garden. There were many beautiful shrubs and we counted at least four gardeners working hard. 'Goodness, Tod would like it here,' Tessa said, 'everything's so well kept.' Shaw had told us there was a magnificent arboretum with huge trees from New Zealand, Japan and China. We did not like to wander too far in case Shaw wanted to leave.

A few of the children had decided to play hide and seek, and I asked if we could join in as it looked great fun. A small pretty girl came up and said, 'We only play with children we know, and we don't want you,' and she marched off with her nose in the air. Kits shouted something extremely rude after her and they all rushed indoors in high dudgeon. We made tracks for the MG and sat and waited . . .

'I don't remember parties being like this,' I said. 'Nobody seems to be in charge.' We stared at the stone lion facing the entrance to the house. The rhododendrons were so magnificent they made Mena's look quite poor in comparison. Suddenly the children came streaming out of the house again and disappeared round the drive with two angry dogs chasing them, and Mrs Carlyon appeared shouting loudly, 'Come here, you bloody hounds!' She looked at us and asked Tessa what we were doing there. 'Go away, all of you, this is a private house. How dare you hang around here!' We looked at her in amazement, feeling very uncomfortable. We crept nearer to the MG and, to our great relief, Shaw came round from the back of the house with Noël Langley. 'Oh, there you are. Enjoying yourselves, darlings?' she asked.

Mrs Carlyon screwed up her eyes. 'Do you know these children?' she asked Shaw.

Shaw flipped her cigarette end into a flowerbed. 'Don't be silly. You invited them, they're Daphne's children,' and she laughed, opening the car door. 'Say thank you, all of you,' she said, sliding her tall frame into the driving seat. We muttered something and Mrs Carlyon, hands on hips, looked nonplussed.

'You should have come to tea,' she said, 'plenty of grub,' and she turned back into the house. We thought her remark very odd, considering she had served us herself.

Shaw made a face at us. 'Well, you're a feeble lot going off on your own like that, just like your mother.'

Back at Mena I made a beeline for the kitchen and tucked into a few rounds of bread and dripping. I went up to tell Tod about the party. She was very upset that we had not made a few friends. 'You missed a real opportunity to get to know some children, other than the honks around here. Mena could do with some jollying along.'

Kits and I thought otherwise. 'Silly, mincy girls, in their fancy dresses, quite useless at climbing trees,' I said and we went out and knocked in the stumps for a game of cricket.

CHAPTER THIRTEEN

As we grew older, Kits and I were allowed to stay on our own with Granny Browning at Rousham. We loved visiting Granny and were very fond of the house. Coming through the front door the scent of lavender was overpowering and, mixed with the smell of apple-wood fires, the lovely fragrance would stop us in our tracks and we would stand sniffing, waiting for Granny to appear to welcome us.

Granny was gentle and gracious with soft, white hair, a flawless pink and white skin which felt like silk, and deep blue eyes that could look ever so sad at times and suddenly light up with merriment. She had been widowed at a very young age and, having adored her husband, had led a lonely and very sheltered life since his death. Her clothes were still rather sombre, though she did wear gay, brightly coloured shawls. There were always pearls at her throat and pretty drop earrings dangling from her pierced ears.

Granny would take us into the garden 'to let off steam' as she put it, after our long journey. Then we would go into the dining-room for tea served by Rosa-bell, who had looked after Granny for years. Rose was small and dark with a pronounced hump on her back. She had very frizzy hair and wore gold gypsy-like earrings, and spoke with a strong cockney accent. She was delighted to see us, and gave us a sumptuous tea. In the dining-room was a cuckoo-clock and as usual Granny gave us a warning not to touch it. We never did; but whenever we went to stay it always stopped. Granny was very kind, but she did not really believe us. Aunt Grace, who lived with her, certainly didn't, and would get quite cross when she arrived down for breakfast to find the clock had ground to a halt in the night.

Aunt Grace had left London and now farmed at Rousham. She had taken up this in middle age, having retired from her work with The Girls' Brigade which she organised and ran during the war years. We were in awe of Aunt Grace; her dark eyes and stern manner quelled any naughtiness in us and I think it was her great fondness for Tess, forever singing her praises, which kept me from trying to get close to her, put off by her formal attitude towards me. It was a pity for she had an excellent brain, was much travelled and had a wonderful memory. She lived to be ninety-two.

Aunt Grace kept pigs and Granny grew very fond of them. She would take us out to the walled garden where they were kept in their sty. She had a great favourite called Pearl, and we would feed apples to her and Granny would scratch Pearl's back with her walking stick. 'Pigs are very clean creatures if you look after them well and respect them properly,' she told us, and indeed the pigs looked very fresh in their spotless pen.

If it happened to be summer when we were visiting, Granny would have her evening swim. At the bottom of the garden was a wood with a dark, deep, rather smelly dew pond. It was usually covered in fallen leaves and other bits of vegetation. Granny would march bravely across the lawn dressed in a warm pink dressing-gown with Kits and I skipping at her side. At the pool she would slowly disrobe, handing us the gown and a towel. Then, resplendent in an old-fashioned black bathing-dress and spotted muslin bath-cap like Miss Muffet, Granny would step daintily into the shadowy water, her white skin gleaming. Like some strange swan she would seem to glide across the silent water, sweeping away the leaves on either side of her. The pond must have been freezing, for no sun ever penetrated the thick trees. Back and forth she went, giving out little sighs of pleasure. She swore it did her good and as she lived until her eighties, I'm sure it did no harm to her. We would sit on her towel and watch the trains go by in the distance on the other side of the River Cherwell beyond the wood.

In winter it was very cold at Rousham. There was no central heating upstairs; we froze in our bedroom and the loo was arctic, so we used to pee in the basin in our room. We would often get sore throats and colds. Even in the lovely blue and white drawing-room the only heat to be got came from two logs balanced against each other over white ash in the fireplace. Granny didn't seem to notice the cold for she wore layers of wool shawls and thick, ribbed stockings, but she did get a little cross with Rosabell during meal-times, ringing the small silver bell on the table a bit too vigorously and stamping her little feet on the floor: 'Come, come, Rosabell, we wish to return to the warmth of the fire.'

Granny had become very religious and after lunch she would lie on the sofa wrapped in a rug and we would sit on footstools by her side and she would talk to us. She told us that the Virgin Mary would sometimes come and visit her and talk to her. 'She is a great comfort to me, and if I am a little fussed about something she tells me not to worry,' she said. 'You see, I knew dear Tommy, your father, would be safe during the war because the Holy Mother told me so.' We sat entranced and as dusk fell the drawing-room would glow softly in the firelight and we would look quietly around us in the hope of a visitation. Granny wrote many letters which she addressed to 'Our Lord', and when she died hundreds of these letters were found, tied up with pink ribbon. I think they were really written to her dead husband, Freddie Browning.

The spell would be broken by Rosabell turning on the lights and taking us off to the kitchen for our high tea. We would sit in the large, comfy kitchen with its warm Aga. Rosabell would have laid a red checked tablecloth at one end of the scrubbed table and we ate boiled eggs and Marmite soldiers and drank good, frothy milk from Aunt Grace's cows. Rosabell would sit watching us, seated in a big sagging chair in her black dress and white cotton apron, a fat tabby cat called Minty on her lap. Rosabell had a high nasal laugh which at times provoked the most awful giggles in Kits and me. Supper and breakfast were also taken in her presence and we often had to splutter our way through our meals. Aunt Grace sometimes came in while we were eating, and one look from her dark eyes quelled any rising mirth in us.

In Granny's bathroom was a large cut-glass bowl full of lavender-scented talcum powder. A snowy white, fluffy puff lay on top of the lid. We used to hide tiny presents for Granny in this jar and then wait outside the door to hear her squeaks of surprise at her discovery.

My grandfather's sister, Great-Aunt Helen, also lived at Rousham. She was confined to a wheelchair most of the time, following an accident to her back as a child, and she had her own set of rooms in a wing of the house. Aunt Helen was very dark, with pitch-black eyes. Her hair was waist-long and done in a loose bun. She wore navy silk dresses to her ankles and always had a black velvet ribbon round her throat with a cameo brooch attached, and fine Queen Mary lace covering her neck and shoulders. She was very sweet and laughed a lot, throwing her head back and giving forth a raucous cackle. At Christmas and birthdays she gave us a 2/6d postal order. She was looked after by a stout lady called Mrs Gossling who had a finger missing on her left hand. Aunt Helen lived for jigsaw puzzles. She did them day in, day out, assisted by Mrs Gossling. Wooden rails had been made on the back stairs and all round the walls of her rooms and the passages to help her in her attempt to walk, which she could do very bent and lame.

It was after one of these lovely holidays at Rousham that Kits went off to his prep school for the first time. In September 1949 he was taken by Bing and my father to West Downs, near Winchester, the school my father had enjoyed so much. Poor Bing was inconsolable. She returned from London the day after seeing him off, her eyes red-rimmed with crying. Tod did what she could to cheer her up, but nothing seemed to help. About four days later she received her first letter from him. In case the headmaster, Mr Tindall, read his letters, Kits and Bing had arranged a code-word for him to use if he was hating school. The code-word was 'it's like your *case* here' – referring to Bing's court case in America.

I went to say good morning to Bing just after she had received her post. With tears pouring down her cheeks, she handed me the little scrappy letter: 'Dear Mummy, hope you are well. It's like your case here. Ask Tod to send jam and cake. I have no friends yet. Love, Kits.'

Piffy came to lunch that day and I can remember Bing leaning out of the window of her bedroom and greeting her sister with a cry. 'Kits loathes his school and is dreadfully unhappy. What am I to do?'

'Pull yourself together for a start,' Piffy shouted back and, turning to me, said, 'What a fuss. I expect he is enjoying himself and just wrote that to work her up.'

It was untrue. For a long while poor Kits did hate school. He had never been away on his own before or known any other little boys his own age, and he found it very difficult to adjust. I regret to say I did not miss Kits very much to begin with. It was bliss being at Mena on my own, with the freedom to come and go as I wished without having to cope with Kits' games and plans for the day. Tod and I would do lessons in the morning and in the early afternoon I would ride Joey for an hour or so, and then Tod and I would take sketching things and a picnic tea and wander about until we found a suitable view. We had several favourite spots that we kept secret, which made it more fun. There was a particular place we liked on the far side of the lakes down at Pridmouth, high up on a hill surrounded by bright yellow gorse. The vista was a panoramic scene of the lakes, the so-called 'happy valley', and Pridmouth cottage and beyond, the wide, sandy bay and sea and Gribbin Head.

As we sketched Tod would talk about her life before she came to us and I thought what an exciting time she had spent and no wonder she grumbled about her dull days at Mena with no 'folk' to see and talk to. In the mid-1930s she had been governess to Lord Furness, and I heard about his children, Dick and Avril. She talked of the Prince of Wales who was often a guest at the house, being keen on Lady Furness, and how they all went hunting on the most superb horses. Tod had never been much struck by the Prince: 'Always an infernal cigarette in his mouth, though he had charm, you could see that.' She had then been governess to the last Sultan of Constantinople, and had lived in a harem. She had stood no nonsense there: 'I soon showed them who was in charge.'

Now that Tod had only me to teach she decided to take over the cooking of Bing's dinner in the evenings. Tod adored her food and had learnt to cook while living in Provence with a family. Bing and I would be sitting in the Long Room reading the papers when we would hear the door of Tod's flat shut firmly and the sound of measured footsteps coming along the passage. Bing would glance up from her reading and catch my eye, groaning. She dreaded these little dinners. 'All I want is a bit of cold meat and an apple,' she would sigh. Tod would come into the room dressed in her crisp white overall, her face set, and hand Bing a menu written in French. 'Here you are, Daphne,' she would say in her no-nonsense voice, and I would bury my face, giggles below the surface.

'Goodness, Tod, I'll never be able to eat all this,' Bing would reply, face alight with apprehension. Tod would ignore such remarks and call me sharply to come and help her find the 'needful'. This was all Tod's favourite wooden spoons and small knives that poor Mrs Burt put away in different places. Little did Tod know that half of her delicious offerings ended up in the rhododendron bushes, Bing creeping out after dark to dispose of the unwanted food. It is odd to think we all ate our supper alone: I still had mine, fruit, in the nursery and Tod had hers up in the flat. I never questioned the routine, happy to read a book until it was time for bed.

Bing always had a book brewing in her mind and as soon as she had finished and published one she was busy writing the next. In 1949 she wrote a novel, *The Parasites*, and a play called *September Tide*. She would spend all morning in her hut and in the afternoon she would be free for an hour or so to go for a walk.

It was about this time in my life, at the age of twelve, that for a short while I became completely obsessed with Bing. Although I didn't spend much time in her company, for she liked to be alone whenever possible, I hated it when she went away. Even a night or two up in London was enough to fill me with dread. I can remember sitting in a fir tree near her hut, praying for hours that she wouldn't go to stay somewhere with my father. She didn't on that occasion, for he fell and sprained his wrist, but there were other days when I felt miserable, never daring to tell Tod, and of course never letting on to Bing herself, for she would have mocked and said how foolish I was. I did once say that if she died I might as well too, for life would be pointless without her. She looked so astonished. 'Good God,' she exclaimed, 'what an odd thing to say. Of course you wouldn't die too, you would just have to get on with things,' and her tone was casual, very matter-of-fact, and her face became inscrutable and I felt rebuffed and rather silly.

I enjoyed our walks, usually accompanied by Mouse, the West Highland terrier given to us by Gillian Carlyon. Wrapped up against the chill wind we would set off across the fields, armed with stout sticks to feel more boyish, and we would make for the Gribbin via Pridmouth beach, striking off up the steep hill, and pausing to look back to the grey slate of Mena in the far distance. Bing would tell me how, as a girl, she had done just that and wondered what house it was that lay buried among the thick trees. She'd been told it was Menabilly: 'Who would have thought that I should live there one day.' She would sometimes talk about a character in the book she was writing, about how she would start thinking like that person and pretend to be them. 'Helps one to get through the day,' she would add. And I would tell her of the strange dreams I had and she, interested, would try to analyse them, wondering what the psychologist Jung would have made of them, for she was deep into his books. She would explain what Jung called the 'collective unconscious' and we would call our conscious and unconscious self number one and number two. 'You must always keep the two balanced,' she said, and later wrote many letters to me on the subject when I was away at boarding-school.

We would come back through the fields, ending up in Mena's grounds, often walking down the Palm Walk, a lovely grassy path, flanked by many waving palm trees, sturdy cedars and tall, smooth-barked eucalyptus. We might pause to pick some green foliage for the many flower vases in Mena. In spring and summer the walk was alive with colour – wild raspberry bushes with their purple fruit and the rhododendron 'Idealist' with its mass of pale cream, bell-like flowers.

The gardens at Mena were at their best in spring, alive with rich green ferns, bluebells and vast patches of snowdrops. In the old days the gardens had been famous for their beauty, and part of them had been used as a nursery for Kew Gardens. We did still come across the odd variety: a sudden splash of scarlet, an exquisite scent wafting through the warm air. At the top of the Palm Walk stood a magnificent double cherry tree which, in early spring, was like a large fluffy pink cloud with a soft, pink carpet beneath. Tod painted many pictures of the tree, and Bing would pick branches and festoon the rooms at Mena.

I would try to delay Bing going indoors, for once there she would no longer be mine, but more distant, thinking of her cup of China tea and the papers, and then back to the hut for more writing – 'prep' she called it, 'like yours with Tod' – and there she would stay till seven, then home, change and drinks.

At weekends when my father came down from London I was sometimes asked to have supper with them in the Long Room. This proved a mixed blessing. Sitting in my pyjamas I would try and follow their conversation about his days in London and people I had never heard of. They would laugh and tease each other: 'Silly Duck, wake up, of course you know Freddie Gough . . . I had dinner with Douglas Fairbanks, sent his love . . . Margot is doing a new ballet. I brought the music, wonderful, she wants me to teach her to shoot with a bow and arrow.' Their talk swept over me and I was glad when Bing said, 'Your bedtime, lovey.'

Kits being away at school had given me much more time to ride and take it all a little more seriously. I had been going regularly to the riding school at Sticker and had taken part in one or two gymkhanas and even won a few minor cups. My father and I had built some jumps in Joey's field and Jimmy Husband and I would take the pony over these. I was riding Joey one day in the park when he stumbled and fell, sending me careering over his head. We got up, shaken, but all right. It happened again trotting round to his stable.

My father was with me at the time and, looking at Joey's grazed knees, said that I was to keep a keen eye on him as he thought he had become a 'stumbler'. Indeed poor Joey had. The vet said he would be unsafe to ride, but was in good health otherwise. This was a blow. After some weeks we decided to part with him and sold him to a milkman down Par who would put him between the shafts of his milk cart, as the vet said he would be unlikely to fall when harnessed up.

I was now horseless. My father was as upset as I was, and wrote to his friend, the great horseman, Joe Dudgen, in Ireland to see if he could find a horse suitable for me to hunt. Within weeks a horse was found. Speedwell arrived over from Ireland and was sent to be schooled by Miss Stocker, ready for the coming hunting season. Speedy, fifteen hands and aged six, was a beautiful half thoroughbred. She was a bay and very pretty to look at, with a sweet temperament.

My first day's hunting was tremendously exciting, but I was disappointed that Miss Stocker didn't let me ride Speedy. 'I want to see how she behaves first,' she said. I had to ride the horrid little Peter with his funny docked tail and mane. He pulled like mad and got thoroughly out of control and barged into the Master's horse. The Master was the renowned Mr Williams, and I shall never forget his look of rage and terrible language. Speedy behaved beautifully and was much admired by Miss Stocker's cronies. We had set out from Sticker at an early hour, for we had a fair way to box. It had pelted with rain, which Miss Stocker said was bad for scent. Bing had bought me a very smart dark hunting jacket of which I was so proud, and I wore a new shirt and Pony Club tie. The rain never let up all day and my new heavy riding mac got soaked through.

I had never ridden over banks before and went over

quite a few at such a rate, right on the heels of Speedy, that I was the other side before I knew it. Peter would jump anything in sight and when we landed would buck with pleasure at his brilliance. Tod had made me some egg sandwiches which I had thrust into my mac pockets, and I remember stuffing them into my mouth as we galloped across the Cornish countryside, the rain stinging my eyes and Miss Stocker yelling at me to 'hold back'. At the kill I was duly blooded and refused to wash my face for days, much to Tod's disgust.

That season I hunted whenever Miss Stocker could spare the time to take me, but as she seemed to be without a suitable mount I had to let her ride Speedy. I never did hunt on my own horse. I got used to Peter's ways and would rather have hunted on him than not at all. When we brought Speedy out to Mena, she proved to be more of a handful than expected. If I missed riding her for more than one day she was so fresh that she would shy at everything in sight. She hated going in the woods and would snort and stand trembling until I turned her for home. I rode mostly in the park and in the fields towards the Gribbin. Jimmy Husband had left school and I hardly saw him now. I found riding rather lonely and was a little afraid of Speedy. She was the devil to catch in the field, and I would spend ages traipsing round after her. Mr Burt was a great help and advised me over her feeding and welfare. Although she jumped splendidly in the hunting field, she was difficult to school over my home-made jumps, even with my father's help. Perhaps I was simply growing out of the horsey stage.

About a year after I had her I was riding Speedy through the farmyard when she suddenly shied at a stationary tractor. I went hurtling over her shoulder and hit my head on a stone water-trough. How long I lay on the ground I do not know, but when I got up Speedy was standing over me looking most concerned. I had a big swelling on my forehead but I remounted and headed for home. At the bottom park gates the postman was pushing his bike and I realised that I was seeing two of him. After putting Speedy in her stable I went and found Bing and told her about my fall. 'Oh darling, how Mrs Brown. Go and find Tod, she'll know what to do.' This I did and was made to lie in a dark room. I had an awful headache for a couple of days, but was then none the worse except that I didn't really enjoy riding as much as I had, and when a year later I followed Tessa to boarding-school I made no real objection when Bing suggested that Speedy should be sold. We sold her to a farmer on the north coast and she went on to win a few points, much to our satisfaction. We went and watched one or two and it was a great thrill. Bing even had wild hopes of the Grand National.

CHAPTER FOURTEEN

It was Ellen Doubleday who suggested to Bing that I should be sent to boarding-school. On one of her visits she had observed to Bing that I was becoming set in my ways 'like a little old lady. She needs girls of her own age and some fun,' Ellen said.

'I don't think so,' said Bing, 'Flave loves being here without the others. She and Tod get on so well.'

'That's just what I mean. She is getting like Tod, complaining about the food and being too serious.'

I heard all this while eavesdropping outside the Long Room door. I could not bear the idea of school and having to leave Mena. Tod didn't relish the thought of my being sent away either, but Aunt Grace was approached. She was friendly with the Mother Superior at St Mary's, Wantage. So it was arranged that I should take the common entrance exam.

Foy Quiller-Couch, the daughter of the writer, 'Q', was asked if she would come and oversee while I sat the paper. She was a JP and thought a sensible person for there were strict rules about this. Foy was a good friend of Bing and we had all had a great time with Foy. At one time she had had a pony and jingle and we used to go on outings in this pony cart, and had even harnessed Joey to it.

The day of the exam arrived and Foy and I sat in the playroom, she at one end of the room and I at a desk near the door. There were strict instructions that on no account must there be any talking. The first paper was English grammar. Tod and I had slogged at this for the last few weeks, having rather neglected the subject of late in favour of English literature. I struggled manfully and was able to finish within the allotted time. Foy then handed me the maths paper. Since the dreaded Miss R, the schoolmistress who had taught us privately during the war, I had developed an absolute blind spot in this subject, and Tod had at first slaved away, trying to din something into me. Alas, it was like hitting a brick wall. She finally gave up the unequal struggle and we did more history instead. The maths paper might as well have been Chinese. I could not make head nor tail of it. Foy, glancing at me from time to time, became agitated that I was not writing at all. I raised my hands in mock despair and she came over and looked at the paper. Her eyebrows shot up and she took the paper to the window to get a better look. Although the daughter of a very brilliant writer and scholar, Foy had had to teach herself to read and write and was not *au fait* with the world of mathematics. If the paper was Chinese to me, it was double-Dutch to her. She broke the silence. 'I think there must be some mistake here,' she said. 'The questions make no sense at all. I think you should write a short note telling them that the paper is complete nonsense.' So we composed a brief letter to the examiners telling them just that.

Bing and Tod were anxious to know how I had got

on, but Foy told me not to say very much, so at lunch I was very quiet. They did demand to look at the questions and I saw Tod's face fall as she studied them. 'Well, Flave darling, we can only go on hoping.' I was very relieved to hear Bing say that she didn't understand one single word of the maths. 'Total blank there,' she laughed.

Weeks went by; we didn't hear a word about the results and I thought it better not to ask. But one day Bing said casually, 'Did I tell you, Sister Janet wrote to say the school is full to overflowing, and they haven't a place at the moment.' She made no mention of the exam. I was relieved and so was Tod and we settled down to lessons again, the emphasis on history and English literature.

The year 1949 was an eventful one for Bing. Her play, *September Tide*, was to be produced in the West End with her friend Gertrude Lawrence taking the leading role. They had been introduced by Noël Coward when my mother was fighting her case in New York, and when Bing was writing her play she had Gertrude in mind to play the main character and so she was thrilled when Gertrude agreed to take on the part. The play was to be directed by the producer Irene Brown, wife of the writer and theatre critic, Ivor Brown. She had also produced Bing's play, *The Years Between*.

When Gertrude Lawrence arrived in London, Bing went up to stay for several days to watch rehearsals and to entertain Gertrude and her husband, Richard Aldridge. Gertrude had brought Bing masses of her cast-off clothes – nothing as smart as Ellen Doubleday's, but rather some lovely jeans and shirts and boyish jackets. Bing was delighted and gave Tessa and me some. I remember a few years later, when I had been presented at Court, wearing some of Gertrude's cocktail dresses to drinks parties; they did look very theatrical and my friends thought I had a rather outrageous dress-sense.

At the beginning of the holidays I travelled up with Bing to London to collect Kits off the school train and to go to see *September Tide*. We were so excited. My father took us to the Savoy Grill for lunch. He had been made a director of the Savoy Group and we always had the most marvellous star treatment. When I was seventeen and sharing the flat with my father, he would take me to his beloved ballet, and we would go and dine together afterwards at the Grill, and I always felt so proud sitting with him. He would be dressed in a beautifully cut suit and spotless cream silk shirt. Lunch with my father was a real treat and it was fun walking into the restaurant with him. People stared at him so. He was extremely good-looking and seemed to know everyone. One or two folk would come up to our table – 'Why, hello Boy, got your family with you. How lovely to see you, Daphne, able to tear yourself away from your beloved Cornwall?' and so forth. We would sit basking in reflected glory.

September Tide was a very adult play about a woman falling in love with her son-in-law – way above our heads – but we enjoyed it very much, firstly because of Gertrude, and secondly because we loved the setting. The main scenes took place in a lovely drawing-room. The set designer had gone down to Ferryside and faithfully copied the sitting-room, even down to the stable-type door looking out to the harbour. Watching the play one expected Gran to make an entrance at any moment. As the curtain fell, we rose to our feet and shouted for the producer for we wanted to clap Irene Brown. She did creep on briefly, puce with embarrassment. We all trooped round back-stage and were introduced to the cast. Michael Gough, who had played the role of the son-in-law, was great fun and took us on the stage and we sat on the sofa and poked our noses into everything. It was the first acting part for a young boy called Bryan Forbes, and I remember being much taken by his wonderful enthusiasm. Gertrude told Bing that he had a great future, and how right she was. We were given tasty crumpets for tea and then Gertrude told us to be off as she wanted to rest before the evening performance. We came away starry-eyed and covered with a mass of Gertrude's stage make-up. Back at Whitelands House my father recoiled when he saw me. 'Good God, the Old Gump looks like a fifty-year-old tart in that get-up,' he said, a remark that promptly brought me down to earth.

Now that we were older, Kits and I were no longer sharing a room. Hank's/Nanny's room was done up for me, and as it had a door into the old night nursery, Kits and I could call through to each other. My bedroom had become a shrine to the film star, Gregory Peck. I was madly and deeply in love. Poor Kits had been dragged off to see his films and I had written to his fan club and got masses of photographs of him, which I pored over and kissed. Tessa, who was now sixteen and really lovely to look at, thought I was even more touched in the head than she remembered. She had also moved bedrooms, to a small bright room over the front door next to Bing's bathroom. Her room was lined with books, read by me when she was away at school, and on the walls she had prints of the Laughing Cavalier and the Mona Lisa, plus one or two school photos.

Tessa loved St Mary's and was doing well there. She had won the verse speaking competition and was thought to have some acting talent. There was talk that perhaps she might go to an acting school when she left Wantage. She had been asked to dances and here Gertrude Lawrence's dresses had come to the rescue. In the summer holidays she spent as much time as she could sailing, and on Wednesdays and Saturdays raced in *Shimmer*, my father keeping an eagle eye, nipping about in *Yggy*, never letting the yacht out of his sight though pretending not to. Tessa was in very good hands with Dick Bunt, but my father was very 'Mrs Brown' on racing days.

Tessa and I were getting on a little better now. She wouldn't jump down my throat quite so often, but she disliked me coming into her room in case I fiddled with things, her make-up and clothes. I had a field day when she was away.

On hot summer days we occasionally went on supper picnics. We had discovered a lovely secret cove down over the cliffs overlooking St Austell Bay and Par with its china clay docks. We had quite a scramble to get to our 'private beach', but it was worth it. There was a splendid deep channel of water with a tiny strip of sand at low tide, with smooth grey rocks on either side and a green velvet patch of grass at the top on which we would lay out our delicious feast of cold chicken and ham, fresh cos lettuce and radishes, with ripe juicy peaches for afters.

We would swim naked and then lie in the last rays of the sun, Bing and I always nut brown, mocking Kits and Tessa their lily white skin. It never bothered us seeing each other naked – we had seen Bing in her bath since we were tiny and Kits and I often shared a bath until our teens. My father did not come on these outings for he disliked swimming in cold water. Only once do I remember him getting into the water.

He had taken us out in *Yggy* and we were having tea anchored off a little beach called Atlantic Bay. It had been a boiling hot day and we had swum off the side of the boat. Suddenly my father announced that he was going to swim. We looked in amazement at each other. 'Ducky, I shouldn't if I were you,' Bing said, trying to hide her smile.

'I suppose you think I can't; well, let me tell you I can swim like a fish and I'm also a bloody good diver.' With that, he disappeared into *Yggy*'s tiny cabin and emerged minutes later still wearing his lightweight summer vest and a pair of ancient silk running-shorts, much frayed about the edges. His legs were thin and unbelievably white. We stared in fascination as he climbed on to the higher deck and stood flexing his arms on the edge. Even Dick Bunt held his breath. My father launched himself off and landed with a terrific splash in the sea, a real belly-flop. He struck out away from the boat in a very fast crawl and I must say we were all very impressed by his style. He circled *Yggy* twice and then, with Dick Bunt's help, heaved himself up the little ladder, his hair sleek and shining like an otter. The water had made his shorts completely transparent and we fell about laughing. Dick Bunt had to turn away to look out to sea, his shoulders shaking with merriment. My father couldn't really see what was so funny and, rather peeved, went to dress. As we chugged back to the harbour he sat looking smug, chain-smoking and taking rapid sips of sloe gin.

Boating did not take up all my father's time. He loved archery and was a good shot. He had taught Bing and they both had their own bows and sets of arrows and had put up a huge professional target on the side lawn.

Kits and I loved watching them, especially when he used his hugely sharp-tipped arrows. Thwack, thwack, they would go, and we would keep the score. He was a dead-eyed dick, nearly always hitting the bull's eye. Round the back of the house, above what once was a coach-house, was a room almost sixty-foot long, and my father put up some targets there. The place was called the Noise Room because we were allowed to play there and make as much din as we liked. One day Tod came to see what we were all doing and my father told her to go and stand behind his targets while he fired on them. It was quite safe, he insisted, she couldn't be hit. Tod eyed him, observing the lethal-looking arrows. 'I think it would be foolhardy; not a very nice invitation if I may say so,' Tod said. My father winked at us. 'Nonsense, my dear Tod, it's very good for you to know what it is like to be under fire. Just imagine what it was like for those poor blighters at Agincourt,' and he took her by the arm and marched her down the room and pushed her firmly behind the targets. Tod stood there bravely and afterwards she came up and muttered to Kits and me, 'You have to humour a madman.'

It was a lovely surprise one weekend when my father said he had invited his great friend Margot Fonteyn down to stay. He told Bing not to panic and that he would organise it all and arrange the menus for he knew what she liked. The object of her visit was for him to show her how to shoot with a bow and arrow for the ballet she was planning called *Silvier*.

Margot arrived on the night-train and the first time we met her was at breakfast. It was laid for her out in the garden. A white cloth was spread on the garden table and she sat drinking fresh orange out of a cut-glass tumbler, my father hovering with the silver coffee-pot, like a cat with two tails. He introduced us and I remember thinking how tiny she was, her huge, dark eyes smiling up at him and her black hair loose, halfway down her back. She wore black slacks and a green checked shirt like a lumberjack's, and as she sat she turned her ankles round and round, as if exercising them. I was riveted and stood staring for some time.

My father took her down to the park and showed off a little with his Turkish bow, shooting the arrows high in the still air till they were lost to sight. One or two became stuck at the top of trees, quivering in the branches, but for once my father didn't mind. He gave her Bing's light bow to try with a collection of new arrows. She looked small and fragile as she stood there, her dark hair lifted by the breeze, and from sideways on her waist was minute, like a child's. She did well, and although the arrow did not travel very far, her style was lovely to see, which of course was all that really mattered for the ballet. They were well pleased with their morning and after lunch my father took her into Fowey and aboard *Yggy* to 'blow the London cobwebs away', he said.

My father had written a ballet based on the opera, *Maid of Orleans*, written in 1881 by Tchaikovsky. He and Margot had discussed it at length and she said how much she would like to play the part of Jeanne d'Arc if it were ever produced. They had high hopes of Benjamin Britten, Leonard Bernstein or Vaughan Williams doing the score, with Oliver Messel the sets, and Ninette de Valois and Frederick Ashton the choreography. Nothing ever came of their great plans, though, and the ballet remained filed away in my father's desk. He was very disappointed, having taken endless trouble writing it and meeting with all the people concerned. He became quite an expert on ballet and went whenever he could to see Margot dance, and I recall that when I was at school she wrote and congratulated me on passing a ballet exam.

In the early 1950s my mother would often go and stay with Gertrude Lawrence at her home in California. Tod and I would be left in charge of Mena, and it was during these times that I found my life rather lonely, missing Bing a great deal. There was no television, but I listened to the wireless a lot, Dick Barton being a must, and I read for hours, deep into the *Hornblower* books and Violet Needham.

I would walk for miles in the Mena woods; they held a magic for me even on the wettest days. With Mouse, the dog, at my heels, I explored every inch of them and we had the place to ourselves, never meeting a soul. High on a wooded hill on the far side of Southcott, hidden by thick laurels and fallen leaves, Bing and I had discovered a large granite monument with the Rashleigh coat-of-arms and names and inscriptions engraved on it. Bing became very excited and we set to and cleared it. Bing was to refer to it in her book *My Cousin Rachel* for, like me, Philip would go and sit there. It became a favourite spot of mine. I would sit with Mouse at my side, overcome with a blissful feeling that no one in the whole wide world knew where I was. It was a sensation of such freedom, with just the birds singing, a twig crackling here and there and, if I peered hard, I could see a faint curl of smoke trailing up from Southcott's chimney. In the far distance, behind me, could be heard the high note of a farmer calling in his cows to be milked and I would know then that it was time I made my way back to the house for Tod would have tea ready.

This was now a daily ritual, taken up in her flat, sitting by the window overlooking the garden. I would shed my boyish swagger of Horatio Hornblower for I was adept at becoming the characters in the books I read – Bing's influence; we would have China tea with condensed milk, thick and creamy, and brown bread with Tod's home-made bramble jelly and delicious, chunky shortbread. After tea we would settle down to read George Eliot's *The Mill on the Floss*, sending tears pouring down our cheeks, or Jane Austen, a much-loved author.

Before going to bed I would wander round the rooms, going into Bing's bedroom to finger her brushes on the dressing-table and dab myself with her scent, Vent Verre. Then I would go to my father's room with its faint whiff of cologne and tobacco in the air. Above his bed hung a large picture of King Arthur kneeling before an altar, an illustration from Sir Thomas Malory's book, *Morte d'Arthur*. It had a quotation written on the bottom of the print: 'For, as I suppose, no man in this world hath lived better than I have done, to achieve that I have done.' Years later when my father lay dead upon his bed, Tessa and I came to pay our last respects to him and I thought how fitting those words were.

Often when Bing happened to be away, my father would come down to Mena on his own for the week-end. We would go into Fowey together, mess about on the boat, taking *Yggy* upriver. We became close during these times alone but on Sunday evenings, long before he was due to depart for London, he would start to mope. His face would become downcast and he would perhaps have a glass of wine too many. I would help him pack his overnight case, watch as he cleaned his shoes to a high polish and lastly put the toy bears in his briefcase, for they always travelled with him. We would sit for a while holding hands for comfort and I think he took a little pleasure from my being there. We would eat a cold supper, the good salad-dressing made by him, and then we would take Mouse for a walk across the lawn towards Bing's hut before the taxi arrived to take him to Par station. He would smile his boyish smile as he waved goodbye, the smoke curling from his ever-present cigarette.

I would lock the door behind him and the silence of the house would be all around me. On the stairs I might linger and glance up at the vast portrait of Bing and her sisters as young girls, and then go slowly up to bed, wishing that she was there. Mena was never the same without her. She brought the place alive with her presence, her cheerfulness and laughter.

CHAPTER FIFTEEN

The most important person ever to visit us at Menabilly was HRH the Duke of Edinburgh. He came to
stay for one night in April 1950. This really set the
house about its ears: everything was spring cleaned
that could be spring cleaned; new glasses were bought
as so many of the wine ones had tiny nicks in them; the
silver was polished until you could see your face in it.
Tod wasn't 'much struck' – 'What a fuss,' she kept
saying, and Gladys, our nice daily, went about muttering, 'Well, *they* are no better than us.' Kits and I were
told to tidy everything in sight and were made to have
our hair cut and washed and our clothes sent to be
cleaned.

Bing was in a state about what she was to wear: 'Oh,
Duck, do I have to put a skirt on?' She made such a
song and dance that my father got fed up and asked his
employer if he minded his hostess remaining in her
favourite get-up. History has not revealed what the
reply was to this odd request, but Bing was assured by
my father that she could do as she wished.

The day dawned and we were told to expect HRH, his valet and private detective. They were going to arrive by private car, self-driven. HRH was to have the Blue Lady room with the detective in a room, also haunted, (I can confirm it), called Little Arthur, just beyond the new bathroom. It became my bedroom as a teenager. The valet was given my father's dressing-room, which had a door into Blue Lady.

Lots of bizarre things happened as we prepared for their arrival. For some strange reason known only to herself, Tod took against the valet before the poor man even set foot in the house and she refused to make his bed. 'He can do it himself,' she declared, and Bing didn't dare insist she make it, for Tod was on the verge of rebellion. My father completely lost his head trying to lay the table for dinner. He suddenly couldn't remember whether you used the cutlery working from the inside or outside or which came first. He had started well, putting lovely flowers in the centre, new mats, side-plates, candles and salt and pepper, and then his mind went blank. He clicked his tongue, ground his teeth and then lost his temper, hurling the cutlery to the floor and screamed at the top of his voice: 'Christ, the bloody things! Why haven't we got a butler? Why is everyone so bloody hopeless in this house? You two get the hell out of here!' This last remark was to us hovering at the door. Tod confused him with telling him what they did in France. 'What the bloody hell have the bloody French got to do with it? Anyway, only honks lay a table that way, silly arse,' he shouted. This last word sent Tod from the room. Bing took no part in all the domestic upheaval, but she did the honours with the flowers, filling the vases with lovely, wild artistic arrangements.

HRH arrived about tea-time and we all met him out

on the gravel. Bing and I did a curtsey, my father and Kits giving a slight nod of the head. There seemed to be endless luggage for so short a visit, and the valet seemed surprised there was no staff to carry the bags; wait until you see your unmade bed, I thought. It was the detective who eventually heaved and sweated with the suitcases while the valet cast his eye about him, soon making demands for an iron and so forth. He was left to the mercy of Tod.

Kits and I were allowed into the drawing-room after tea and we sat quietly in the background. HRH paced the floor in a restless manner, suddenly throwing himself down in a chair and picking up a *Country Life* or yachting paper, leafing through it and then snatching up another. But the talk seemed to be animated and we noticed that Bing was in good form, chatting away and laughing, much more relaxed than the two men. She looked lovely, changing for dinner into one of Ellen's cast-offs. HRH found nothing amiss with the dining-room table as far as we knew, and he ate Mrs Burt's dinner with relish. Tod had to give the valet dinner in her flat which made Kits and me giggle, while the detective had his below stairs in the kitchen.

My father was up at the crack of dawn to lay the breakfast – he would trust no one else. Bing refused once more to conform and had hers as usual in her room, making an appearance later in time to say goodbye.

We gathered once more outside the front door and HRH was much more relaxed, laughing and joking, but Kits and I thought the valet looked pale and drawn. We wondered what Tod and he had talked about the evening before. Goodbyes were said and we were dispatched to open the park gates, tearing off on our bikes. HRH gave us a huge grin as the car swept through and waved his hand out of the window. The valet had left all the rooms immaculate, the sheets neatly folded; it looked as if no one had ever been there.

It was not very long after the royal visit that we had the ornithologist, Peter Scott, to stay. My father had met him on several occasions and shared his love of sailing as well as greatly admiring his work as an artist and writer.

I remember a few days before Peter Scott was due to arrive we were all aboard my father's lovely yacht, *Jeanne d'Arc*, anchored in Fowey harbour. We were eating delicious hot pasties wrapped in white linen napkins. A strong west wind was blowing but Kits and I had escaped the fug in the stuffy cabin and were up on deck breathing in the fresh air. The wind howled through the rigging making an eerie sound and moaned round the cabin skylight which was half-open. 'I say, it's just like *Scott of the Antarctic* up here,' I shouted down to the trio below. Kits and I had been to see the film of that name and were still haunted by it.

My father came darting out of the cabin, the smoke from his cigarette swirling about his head. 'Look you two,' he said, 'you realise we have Captain Scott's son coming to stay so you had better keep remarks like those to yourselves when he is in earshot.' We felt rather snubbed but excited at the prospect of meeting such a person.

Bing had met Peter Scott as a child – they were about the same age – and she recalled him being very blond and dressed in a garment like a Greek tunic. His mother had wanted her son to grow up tough and strong like his father, so even in mid-winter Peter wore thin, light clothes. Kits and I had been fascinated by these tales and dreaded getting the giggles on seeing him for the first time.

He arrived early one Saturday evening, and we hovered in the background while my father and Bing went out to greet him. As he came to be introduced I was amazed by his likeness to John Mills, the actor who had played the part of Captain Scott. Kits and I stared up into a pair of piercing blue eyes set in a tanned face, and with relief we saw that he was dressed in navy-blue sailing trousers and a blue canvas smock, having just come off a friend's yacht in Fowey. Bing and I agreed later when we had a moment alone that Peter Scott was a 'menace' – 'The most attractive eyes, they sort of linger on one, I found myself taking more trouble with my appearance, plus a good splash of scent!' she laughingly said.

The next day my father suggested that we all went sailing in *Jeanne d'Arc*. He was eager to show Peter Scott his boat. The day was rather overcast and not very warm. Bing made our guest put on a dark blue boat cloak with a brass clasp that had once belonged to my Great-Uncle Monty who had been an admiral. Peter looked very dashing, and more so when he topped it with his yachting cap. Bing and I nudged each other in ecstasy at the sight of our 'menace', and my father and Tessa glanced at us suspiciously, raising their eyes heavenwards. Tessa got her own back when we reached Fowey, for Peter took her arm when we all marched through the town to the Fowey yacht club.

The club was teaming with would-be yachtsmen and my father introduced our guest to as many of his cronies as he could find. Kits and I stood by the rail and looked out across the harbour at the hustle and bustle of the many large and small craft making ready to set sail. We could see the blue-green paint of *Jeanne d'Arc* gleaming, her rust-coloured mainsail already hauled up by George, my father's new boatman. We prayed that the sea would be calm.

I suddenly turned round to find Peter Scott standing staring at me in an intense manner, his blue gaze fixed on me. I felt my cheeks redden and I averted my eyes. 'Flavia,' he said, 'I think I would like to draw you, Kits too, perhaps, just head and shoulders.' The strong wind blew the boat cloak about his body and he looked like someone from another century. I longed for Bing to come to the rescue. It was all very well for me to admire my 'menace' from afar but not the thing at all for the 'menace' to ogle me.

Kits and I moved slowly away and then darted down the stone steps to the narrow stretch of rocks below. Thank goodness it was low tide. 'Oh, how awful, how ghastly. I should hate to be drawn, please please let him not,' I said to Kits, who heartily agreed. We could think of nothing worse. We skulked on the rocks until, with relief, we saw George approaching in the rowing-boat to take us all aboard *Jeanne d'Arc*.

We sailed out towards the Gribbin Head and then into Pridmouth Bay where we anchored for lunch. Thank goodness the water was flat and calm in spite of a stiff breeze. Peter again mentioned the idea of drawing me. Bing looked pleased but I could tell both she and my father were puzzled by his choice: why not do Tessa, a far better subject with her pretty looks. But Peter did not suggest it, much to Tessa's irritation: 'Needs his eyes testing,' she said.

It was on the return journey back to the harbour that Peter, having taken a turn at the helm, came and sat with Bing, Kits and me in the warmth of the stern. Bing happened to mention the bats that infested the attics at Mena. Peter's eyes lit up and he asked if he could do a bit of exploring when we got back.

The only access to the attics was through Tod's flat. We had for the moment forgotten her fear and dread of the bats, and when she came to see what was going on her face became set in the look we knew well. She stood barring the way, arms akimbo: 'Please leave well alone. I am not having those filthy creatures disturbed. Daphne, it is too bad of you to encourage such a venture, I really take a dim view,' and she turned away, leaving us standing in awkward silence.

Bing shrugged her shoulders. 'Oh dear, we shall have to think of some way to pacify her. You, Peter, will show an interest in her paintings – she is awfully good, you know,' she said. Heartened by these remarks we followed her through the heavy curtain which shut off the narrow passage leading to the place where the trap-door to the attics was set up in the ceiling of a tiny boxroom.

Bing, Kits and I waited in the dingy room while up above us we could hear the distant sound of Peter moving about, and every so often what seemed to be an exclamation, whether curse as he hit his head on rafters, or joy as he spied a bat, we had no way of knowing. Then for a long time there was silence.

'Supposing he crashed to his doom into the old part of the house. What shall we do?' Bing said, her voice lowered in solemn tones. She climbed up the short ladder to the trap-door and, looking down at us, pretended to fall, her face stricken. Then she called out, 'Peter, are you okay?' There was no reply. 'I had better go and see where he is,' she said, and she started to lift the trap-door.

Kits, his face white in the dim light, went up after Bing and held on to her trouser-leg. 'No, no, you'll crash as well. Leave him, he'll be all right,' he begged. I wondered if Peter had come across any rats, as at one time they had been swarming up there.

At last Peter appeared, his face dusty but with a wide

grin lighting up his features. 'Wonderful,' he said as he closed the trap-door and climbed down. 'Quite, quite remarkable.'

We tramped back into the cheerful brightness of the flat and a curious sight met our eyes. Tod stood in full battle order in her own private war against the bats. Only her face was left uncovered, the rest of her concealed by a black oilskin which enveloped her body, meeting up with stout rubber sea boots and a large shiny sou'-wester pulled well down over her brows. Her hands were encased in thick gardening gauntlets and she held a tennis racket as if it were a sword. Peter Scott stood transfixed. 'My word,' he marvelled, 'you certainly look menacing.' Hearing our code-word for attractive used in its rightful context was too much for Bing. Putting a hand over her mouth to hide her laughter she fled from the scene closely followed by Kits, and I could hear their gales of mirth as they reached the safety of the main landing some twenty yards away.

Peter, not to be defeated by Tod's weird appearance, stepped closer to her side. His shoulders were covered with thick black cobwebs and bits of chalky masonry. He beamed at Tod. 'Look, Miss Waddell, what I have here,' and, fishing in his pocket, he brought out a clutch of black furry objects. There, nestling in the palm of his hand, were two quivering bats. It was with great pride that he stretched out the frail wing of one; the tiny claw-like hooks clung to his fingers and he stroked it with real delight and feeling. Tod gave a strangled cry, dropped the tennis racket and lunged up the step to her sitting-room. The door banged shut making the pictures on the wall shake. 'Ah, well, never mind,' said our intrepid naturalist. 'I was going to let her handle one so she would never be scared again. They are darling little things, and these are beauties, the Lesser Horseshoe bat, what's more.'

Tod was not seen again that evening; in fact, she told me later that she had gone to bed after taking a soothing cup of Bengers and read *The Life of Doctor Johnson*. This was a ritual in times of stress and worked wonders.

The next morning, soon after breakfast, there was no escaping the dreaded sketching session. I was hauled into the Long Room and sat in a high-backed chair while Peter seated himself a little way off, glasses on the end of his nose, artist's block before him, pencil in hand. The first few minutes passed slowly and then I forgot all about being self-conscious. Peter chatted away, telling me all about the expedition he had made to the North-West Territories of Canada, to the River Perry. The object had been to see for himself how the world's waterfowl were faring, the ducks, geese and swans. He was writing a book about it, having kept a journal while on the expedition, and was going to call it *Wild Geese and Eskimos*. 'When the book is published I'll send you a signed copy,' he promised, 'as a reward for letting me draw you.' And indeed he did. For my birthday a year later I received a copy and on the blank space below the title in the front of the book he had painted me two beautiful King Eiders.

Peter Scott also did a drawing of Kits and when Bing and my father saw them they were delighted. Once they were framed they hung on a wall in Bing's bedroom and remained there until her death in 1989. Kits now has them, for we thought it proper that they should remain a pair, for they complement each other, and I think that the artist would have agreed.

At the end of the Christmas holidays in 1950 we all travelled up to London. Bing had been given seats for a matinee of *King's Rhapsody*. This was a great treat for we were to go backstage afterwards to meet Ivor Novello. Tessa and Kits were due back at school the following day for the Lent term and I was to travel down to Mena with Daddy on the Friday. Bing was going to stay with Gertrude in New York where the latter was starring in *The King and I*.

We somehow managed to squash into Whitelands House, Tessa sleeping on a camp-bed in Daddy's tiny dressing-room. Kits' tuck-box took up most of the hall. Thank goodness their trunks had gone to the schools in advance. This was to be Tessa's last term. She was in the lower sixth and now that she was sixteen she wanted to go to France to stay with a great friend of Bing to improve her French.

We simply adored *King's Rhapsody*. The play was set in some mythical Middle European country called Murania, not unlike Antony Hope's Ruretania. We already knew the songs – 'Some Day my Heart Will Awake', 'A Violin Began to Play', and so on. The scenery and costumes were spectacular, and I thought Ivor Novello divine. There was a lovely actress called Vanessa Lea playing the part of the princess.

At the end of the performance we were ushered round to the stage-door and taken along narrow passages until we came to a red door which was thrown open and there stood Ivor Novello, tall and dark with just faint touches of grey at the temples. He was still in his dark green King's uniform and black shiny tasselled boots. His faced was bronzed with make-up and he had red dots in the corner of his eyes – to make them stand out on stage, he told us later. I thought him the most beautiful person I had ever seen. He came forward and threw his arms round Bing. 'Daphne, darling, how wonderful to see you. You look simply lovely.' He took my hand and I gazed into a pair of the darkest liquid brown eyes imaginable. He smiled and his face lit up. My thirteen-year-old heart lurched, and I remember thinking that I would never again see such compelling eyes. He looked down at Kits and ruffled his hair and laughed. 'You'll do,' he said, 'you'll do. Your beautiful daughter Tessa takes after you, Daphne, lucky girl.' We were given glasses of orange juice, and Bing had champagne. He sat back to front on a chair, his chin resting on his folded arms. Bing and he chatted away and I stared about me, seeing his dressing-tables, the bottles, make-up and telegrams stuck at odd angles on the brightly lit mirror. There were spring flowers in many vases, brought up from his house in the country. 'I bring them to remind me of my lovely garden,' he told us.

That evening my father took us to dinner in a restaurant in the King's Road owned by the Whitelands House Management. We were having a very jolly time, my father in one of his good moods, teasing me about my new heart-throb, Ivor Novello. We had finished our main course and were ordering sickly afters when Bing, her face rather sombre, nudged him. He looked at her. 'What's up, Duck?' he asked.

She looked at me, her blue eyes wary. 'It concerns Old Gumpet,' she said. We all sat up and waited. 'This morning Sister Janet rang up from St Mary's, Wantage, and said they had unexpectedly got a vacancy at the school. She apologised for it being so last-minute, but wondered if we would like to send Flavia this term as they might not have room until next year.' She paused, taken aback by our looks of utter amazement and shock.

'Silly old nun,' I laughed weakly. 'As if I would go

just like that.' Kits joined in and we all laughed except Bing who appeared flustered. She quickly drained her wine-glass.

'Well, the thing is—' A long pause. 'I said *yes*. I thought it was an answer to our prayers. Also, it would be nice for Flave to have Tessa there, as it is her last term.'

There was a stunned silence. I felt as if I was going to choke, bile rising in my mouth. 'Prayers,' I said, hardly above a whisper. 'You have been praying for me to go away to school. How could you? How utterly beastly. I won't go. I won't, I won't,' and I burst into tears.

'She can't go,' Tessa said, appalled, 'she has no uniform or anything.'

My father drew deeply on his cigarette. 'It's a bit steep, Duck, such short notice.' He handed me his clean white hanky.

Kits, his face white, tears springing to his eyes said, 'Poor Beaver, school is awful.'

I hardly slept that night. I heard every car going down the King's Road and Kits and I talked about it when he woke early in the morning. 'I shall run away,' I declared, and I thought of our hideouts in the Mena woods. I could live there.

First thing after breakfast, of which I ate nothing, Maureen took me to Peter Jones to buy a skirt and blouses, some rough woolly underclothes plus horrid brown bar shoes, knee socks and two pairs of clumping walking-shoes. I felt sick the whole time and Maureen was very sweet and kind, looking almost as unhappy as I was. Bing said it was silly to buy a new uniform since Tessa had told her it was cheaper to get second-hand stuff at the school.

Tod happened to be in London for a few days seeing 'folk' and came round as soon as she heard the news.

'Flave, darling, what a to-do. We should have done much more work before you went to St Mary's, it's too bad of Bing.' She sat down on the only comfy chair, her face grave, and I started to cry and she, slightly embarrassed, made tut-tut sounds. 'Mena won't be the same without you,' she said, no doubt wondering about her own future now there was no one left to teach. We sat and sewed some of Tessa's name-tapes on my few belongings. Maureen had got a clothes list from the file she kept on the school. The list seemed endless and we looked at it in despair. 'You'll just have to make do and mend for the moment,' Tod said, lips pursed, sewing a name-tape on to Gertrude Lawrence's white silk pyjamas. We borrowed an old heavy leather suitcase belonging to my father, and she packed the clothes.

I had hardly spoken to Bing that morning. She and Tessa had left early to have their hair done and to shop. Mrs Lester, my father's daily, polished my new shoes and grabbed the suitcase, making the leather shine. She bustled around and made coffee for Bing who returned looking smart, hair newly permed. She looked remote to me in her London clothes, a different person, make-up beautifully applied by the woman who came to give her facials each day. She sat on the bed in her room making endless calls to her London friends; I heard her laugh and wondered how she could feel cheerful on such a dooming day. It irritated me and I went and sat in the one and only bathroom, leaning against the towel-rail, staring out at the Duke of York's headquarters, wishing I was anyone but me, wishing I was grown up and miles away, school long forgotten.

Bing called out to me that we would all have to go and have an early lunch, as the school train left Paddington at one thirty sharp. I said I didn't want anything to eat, and I heard her talk to Tod in French so I wouldn't understand. Kits' train was not until much later and he and Bing had planned to spend the waiting time in a cartoon cinema.

We went back to the restaurant of the night before, the dark, gloomy light depressing me further and the smell of greasy food making me feel very unwell. I sat crumbling bits of hard white bun on my plate, the dough sticking in the back of my throat. I couldn't touch the grilled cutlets placed before me.

'Oh, dear, we should have got your hair done or washed at any rate,' Bing said to me. 'It does look a shilling.' (Shilling was our family word for dull, uninteresting.) I looked at Tessa: she too had had a smart hairdo which curled round her lovely face becomingly, and her uniform looked crisp and formal. I saw Bing and Tessa exchange looks and they spoke softly in French for a moment, and for a second I hated them both, tears of self-pity threatening to engulf me. Tessa's 'elle pleur' made me want to rush from the place, out into the noisy King's Road. Instead I sulked, wishing I were dead.

Back in the flat and once more in the bathroom, I wondered who would look after Speedy, who would exercise her and feed her. She could be such a handful. My father, returning to say goodbye, brought me a little to my senses. I ran to him and asked him the questions about my horse. 'Why, old Mr Burt,' he said, 'she's already being taken care of.' I thought of Mr Burt's surprise at my not returning. We all stood in the narrow little hall putting on our coats. My old green one with the once soft velvet collar was way above my knees and Tessa groaned when she saw it: 'Oh, God, what do you look like? The girls will think you're Orphan Annie.' Maureen told her not to be so horrid.

Kits, his face now as white as mine for he dreaded

returning to school, took Bing's hand as we all piled into the lift down to the waiting car. The car, a large Godfrey Davies hire, was drawn up outside. My father and Maureen kissed me goodbye and he gave me ten shillings pocket money which I had seen him borrow from Bing that morning. We climbed in the car and drove out in the heavy traffic. Please God, let the car ʰreak down, please let us miss the train. But we swept down the incline and under the archway and came to a stop at the station.

There were cars and taxis disgorging their occupants, and I saw many girls in brown berets and the brown, pinkish tweed of the St Mary's coats, a few of them carrying lacrosse sticks. A fat porter led us to the platform, the school train already in, its doors flung open, and what seemed to be hundreds of girls scrambling about. The noise was horrific, with shouts and yells and screams of laughter. Tessa soon made contact. 'Hi, Tessa, we have bagged a carriage down here, we've kept a place for you.'

A tall, pleasant girl came up and Tessa introduced her to us. 'Bing, you remember Jill Nichols, we're in the same form.' Tessa explained about my sudden arrival.

Jill looked at my old coat and smiled. 'My sister Judy is here. She's your age. I expect you'll be in the same form, the lower fourth. You can sit in her carriage.'

I stood close to Tessa. 'Can't I sit with you?' I asked.

'Of course not. The seniors don't sit with the juniors.'

Tod stood grim-faced, staring about her. 'What a shindig,' she said.

At that moment a tall nun came up and shook Bing by the hand. 'So this is Tessa's sister. How alike they are,' she beamed at us all. Tessa and Bing looked at each other in amazement, and Tod laughed.

We were ushered further down the platform to where a small huddle of new girls stood and one or two tearful, anxious parents who looked pained and nervous. I eyed the girls and they in turn stared at me. 'I think it's time I settled the new ones on board,' the smiling nun said.

Bing bent and kissed me. 'I'll write from New York, lovey,' she said. 'Tessa will look after you.'

The latter had already gone to join her cronies in another part of the train. Our cases had been stowed away in the guard's van. Tod gave me a hug. 'Take care, Flave darling. I will miss our times together.'

Kits and I looked at each other. 'Bye, Beaver,' he said. I followed the nun into the carriage and took the nearest seat. Six girls sat down, one with tears pouring down her face. We sat in silence. The train shuddered slightly, the whistle blew and we slid slowly out of the dim light of the station into the bright light of the sunny afternoon.

EPILOGUE

I did not enjoy my school days at St Mary's very much, but I did make good and lasting friends. I left at the age of seventeen and went to Paris where I was lucky enough to study art for a while. On returning to London, my father was keen for me to be presented at Court. This I did but was a most reluctant débutante, disliking the frivolous society into which I was thrust.

I lived with my father in his flat at Whitelands House in Chelsea and went to acting school for I had the urge to go on the stage. But when John Gielgud asked me to read for the young girl's part in his 1956 production of *The Chalk Garden* at the Haymarket I refused, much to my mother's vexation, as she thought I was being offered a golden opportunity, an opening into the theatre. To my parents' dismay I had fallen head over heels in love with a young army officer. Much against their wishes I married Alastair two months after my nineteenth birthday. Two years later I had my son Rupert. We lived in London and then in the country until Alastair and I divorced in 1972. I married again in

1981 and now live in the West Country with my husband, Peter, and our cats and dogs.

Tessa, who had married a year or so before me, had two children and now has four grandchildren. She lives with her second husband, David, in London. She and I have become very close and we often laugh at the way we behaved towards each other in our childhood. We both see Kits and his wife, Hacker, and their four children as much as we can, the death of our mother uniting us more closely as the years go by. The autumn of 1993 has been very special for Kits and Hacker. They have moved down to Cornwall to live at Ferryside. They and their children will bring back once more that sense of belonging, a continuation which has been lacking for all of them since my mother died. Ferryside really does belong to the du Mauriers and I am sure that my mother would rejoice at the thought of her son Kits and his family sustaining 'the loving spirit' which she, in her youthful days, brought to the place.

My aunts, Angela and Jeanne du Maurier, are still alive and in their eighties. Tod lived well into her nineties, and remained in good health, and close to the family. She stayed in a flat in Battersea which my mother gave to her on her retirement.

My mother died on 19 April 1989, a month before her eighty-second birthday. She had been unwell for some years and the last two had been especially cruel, with increasing loss of memory and a deep depression taking their toll. I felt the mother and friend I adored had 'gone away' from the family she loved so much shortly after she suffered a mild stroke in the early 1980s. This, coupled with the dreaded writer's block, sealed the fate of her declining years.

I watched with ever-increasing dismay and agony the slow deterioration of the once bright, cheerful and loving 'Bing' into an unhappy, lonely and frightened little soul, taking less and less interest in her family and surroundings. Perhaps it is a du Maurier disease, this dreadful deep gloom and despondency, for Bing's grandfather, George du Maurier, fell victim to melancholia in later life as did his son, Gerald. I witnessed the same with Gran, remembering the visits to see this once beautiful woman, sitting covered in shawls, her face blank as she turned listless eyes upon us as we entered her room, scarcely knowing who we were. And when we left, Bing, worried, her eyes sad, would say, 'Poor, poor Mummy, it is too awful. What a fate. *Never* let me become like that.'

I began writing this short memoir of my childhood two years before Bing died. One day, out of the blue, I suddenly had almost total recall and the urge to write it all down. It was never meant for publication, just something for the family to read. It was an unusual childhood, in some ways idyllic, though there is perhaps a price to pay for having two talented and famous parents. I did adore my mother and came to love my father, both of whom became very close and loving to me in my teens, my most difficult years. I lost the fear I had of my father, something that had dogged my early childhood. I wish so much that he had not died in 1965 at the untimely age of sixty-eight.

I have heard it said that a person only really grows up when both parents have gone; what I do know is that life will never be quite the same again. Cornwall no longer holds that enchantment it once did. Gone is the excitement of driving down those leafy, winding roads to the lovely old houses, my beloved Menabilly, and then later Kilmarth where Bing lived out her years.

I feel I have no 'roots' left, that they were blown away when Tessa, Kits and I scattered Bing's ashes over her chosen spot, above the Cornish cliffs, the fitful April sun shining bright upon the calm and distant sea. A lone gull mewed a final farewell overhead, and as we three stood there we did not mourn, for we knew that our beloved Bing was free at last to go to that 'never never land', where she had always believed that 'Daddy' would be waiting in his boat for her and together they would sail into infinity.